THE NET WORTH WORKOUT

A POWERFUL PROGRAM FOR A LIFETIME OF FINANCIAL FITNESS

SUSAN FEITELBERG

AMACOM AMERICAN MANAGEMENT ASSOCIATION

New York ■ Atlanta ■ Brussels ■ Chicago ■ Mexico City ■ San Francisco
Shanghai ■ Tokyo ■ Toronto ■ Washington, D.C.

Special discounts on bulk quantities of AMACOM books are
available to corporations, professional associations, and other
organizations. For details, contact Special Sales Department,
AMACOM, a division of American Management Association,
1601 Broadway, New York, NY 10019.
Tel.: 212-903-8316. Fax: 212-903-8083.
Website: www.amacombooks.org

This publication is designed to provide accurate and authoritative
information in regard to the subject matter covered. It is sold with the
understanding that the publisher is not engaged in rendering legal,
accounting, or other professional service. If legal advice or other expert
assistance is required, the services of a competent professional person
should be sought.

The opinions, observations, and other statements contained in this book are
those of the author and may not reflect those of JPMorgan Chase & Co. or
its subsidiaries, directors, officers, or employees.

Library of Congress Cataloging-in-Publication Data

Feitelberg, Susan, 1962–
        The net worth workout : a powerful program for a lifetime of financial
fitness / Susan Feitelberg.
            p.   cm.
        Includes bibliographical references and index.
        ISBN 0-8144-7315-6
        1. Finance, Personal.   2. Investments.   I. Title.

    HG179.F393   2005
    332.024' 01—dc22   2005024602

Printing number

10   9   8   7   6   5   4   3   2   1

To my parents,
Sheila and Joe Feitelberg,
who taught me what it means to be happy, healthy, wealthy, and wise.

CONTENTS

Preface: How the Net Worth Workout Was Born   vii

1   The Net Worth Workout Explained   1

2   Attitude   17

3   Your Shape, Goals, and Plans   41

4   Earning: Which Gear Are You In?   71

5   Spending: What Kind of Fuel Are You Burning?   91

6   Saving: How Much Do You Save in a Year?   127

7   Investing: What Shape Are Your Investments In?   149

8   Getting It All Together   179

Appendix A: Useful Websites   203

Appendix B: Useful Financial Planning Tools   209

Glossary   215

Index   223

HOW THE NET WORTH
WORKOUT WAS BORN

WHEN I BECAME AN INVESTMENT ADVISER, I began to look closely at the reasons some people fail to achieve their full financial potential. There were basic things my clients all knew they should be doing to take care of themselves, both physically and financially, yet many weren't doing them. With the abundance of information around, my clients could get financially savvy whenever they wanted to. Yet most of them were falling well short of their prosperity potential. I decided to find out why.

I talked to people who felt overwhelmed all the time.

As I reviewed their savings accounts, CDs, mutual funds, stocks, 401(k)s, IRAs, and other investments, I'd ask them how much money they thought they needed for retirement. I was astonished to discover that, even among my many clients in their fifties and sixties, the typical answer was: "Gee, I really never gave it much thought." Even people who had excelled as bankers, attorneys, professors, managers, or—heaven help us!—economists had hardly considered their own retirement.

Not only had they given financial planning little thought, but when they did make a financial decision, they often chose inadequate sources of information as their guides. Typically, I found, people's expectations were as much a function of others' experiences as of their own. For instance, a buddy or boss had helped them pick the funds they owned. Or they were influenced by a parent: "I dunno . . . Dad always kept his money in CDs." Typically, guidance had come from a "consultant" who didn't even know the person's holdings.

It boiled down to two problems: Most people didn't know precisely where they were trying to go financially, so naturally, they didn't know for certain how to get there.

Even the people in the poorest financial health usually had some vague idea of what they wanted to achieve, but they had never defined their goals in clear terms and they had never sat down to create a systematic plan of action for arriving at those goals. In most cases, they weren't even all that conscious of where they were today. Their financial status frightened them, so they looked at it as little as possible.

These clients needed a way to bring their financial plans into sharp focus. They needed a process that would help them identify the course of action for each step along the way and practical tools for measuring their progress at meaningful intervals.

I began thinking about what kind of people operate on the opposite end of this spectrum. Who knows the most about how to set clearly defined goals? Who has mastered the art of rigorously, ruthlessly pursuing their objectives, of settling for nothing short of victory?

One day the answer came to me: *athletes.*

I knew I'd hit upon the right metaphor because, as a young teen, I'd become a serious athlete and started competing in triathlons. Establishing a series of goals, then achieving them and devising new ones, has been central to my day-to-day life ever since.

In competitive sports, there's a direct link between vision, persistence, and success. The exact same principles that work to help an athlete push herself to victory could help people push themselves toward greater prosperity.

I began developing a system for financial prioritizing, goal setting, and follow-up that tapped directly into the language, metaphors, and mind-set of athletic training. I began to view stamina, strength, conditioning, and even nutrition as metaphors for financial concepts. I developed a system of self-monitoring and goal setting that came directly from athletic competitions, but which worked elegantly in the world of personal finance. The solution initially devised for my clients evolved into *The Net Worth Workout,* a virtual "fitness regimen" for finances.

Since I'd never recommend to others something I haven't tried, I first put myself on the workout. Though the concept struck me as great, I had to be sure it worked, that it was livable. Frankly, the results amazed me, and it had nothing to do with the performance of the market. Inside twelve months, and *despite unchanged earnings,* my savings toward investment increased by 20 percent. Even as my stress level fell, my net worth rose dramatically—a direct result of the increased savings. I also didn't second-guess my investment decisions, because I knew that this combination of increased savings and sound investing would be what I needed to reach my goals.

Since that time six years ago, I've been helping clients achieve similar results. To date, I've put hundreds of my clients on the Net Worth Workout, and after one year, their net worths increased dramatically. And more important, so did their financial peace of mind! Best of all, the Net Worth Workout allowed them to build net worth and feel better about their money *using the financial means they already had.*

Now it's your turn.

In my office in New York City I may do a great deal of good, but this book takes the principles all the way to you. My intention is to guide people toward increased net worth and financial peace of mind, just as I've done with clients. On the Net Worth Workout, you'll become your own "personal financial trainer," gaining financial health, strength, and stamina on a day-to-day basis. For additional information about the Net Worth Workout, go to networthwork out.com.

A C K N O W L E D G M E N T S

THIS BOOK COULDN'T HAVE HAPPENED without the support and insight of so many people. I will always be greatly indebted to these individuals. Coincidentally, when I sat down to write this section, I noticed their backgrounds could be categorized into four key quadrants, the publishing business, sports buddies, work colleagues, and friends and family, in no particular order. Several years ago I spoke to a client, Janis Donnaud, who was with Random House and is now a literary agent. Her receptiveness and encouragement of this idea was an important reason for pursuing it. Billy Fitzpatrick, a freelance writer, reviewed the initial proposal and helped me shape the quadrants. It was particularly delightful because we both happened to be doing this in July and August while in Sag Harbor, a great writers' town in the Hamptons. Carol Schuster and Julie Halpin are terrific friends whose insights from the world of advertising helped me clarify how a book like this could reach a mass audience.

My sports buddies were invaluable sounding boards,

whether it came to discussing concepts or blowing off stress from spending too much time in front of the computer. I think that the last year, for the first time in my life I've spent more time in front of the computer than running, biking, or swimming! Bernadette Taylor, Alistair Rogers, Tiger Williams, Ike and Lesley Groff, and Karen Smyers gave me interesting insights from their expert athletic and financial knowledge as well as their own experiences, all of which added color to these stories. Members of Doug Stern's Masters Swim Team always had interesting questions and helpful advice when we met at the diner after our workout, even though it might be 10 o'clock at night! Although I didn't often make their 5:40 a.m. boathouse bike rides, the members of the Breakfast Club were inspirational in their consistency, teamwork, dedication, and e-mails. Ed Kinnaly, who first encouraged and moved me to pick up this project, knows better than anyone the amount of work that went into it. I will forever be grateful for his empathy, support, and interest. There are lots of other terrific people who deserve thanks, and some who deserve apologies, perhaps, for any boredom I may have caused talking about "the book," particularly those who couldn't easily get away from me, like during a 60-mile bike ride!

My colleagues at work—Andy Ireland, Doug Labrecque, Peter Wall, Robert Corsaire, Jean Forrestal, and Donovan Mannato—were always there to encourage me, particularly when I was burned out or feeling discouraged. Their support helped me see the light at the end of the tunnel and the benefit it held for our business and our firm. Then the folks at the mutual fund companies—John English of Alliance; Lisa Grant of American Century; Amy Perrino, Lisa Kueng, and Maura McGrath of Van Kampen; Rob Mims of GE Capital; Mike Raso and Jean Pissaro at Oppenheimer Funds: They saw the need for a book like this that could help simplify our client's financial lives.

Thanks to the folks at Atchity Entertainment who got behind *The Net Worth Workout* and helped me get it to Amacom. The terrific team at Amacom, Jacquie Flynn, Irene Majuk, Kama Timbrell, Jim Bessent, and Doug Puchowski, made it fun, easy, and so painless, I loved working with you. Jenn Hoefler at Krupp Kommunications was always a step ahead when it came to first-class publicity. Julia Wilson and Rob Kaplan helped me shape *The Net Worth Workout* so it was in its best it could be. A very, very special thanks to my sister Mary, who is one of the most talented writer/editors around. Besides, who else but an older sister would coop herself up for a weekend in a one bedroom apartment in New York City to work on a book? My Uncle Karl Feitelberg was so helpful with endorsements. Finally, my other brothers and sisters and their spouses, John and Polly, Jane and Mike, Rosie and Chris, Mary's husband Peter, and my brother Mark, took an interest in the progress of this project at so many family get-togethers.

I hope you enjoy reading this book as much as I enjoyed working on it. It truly has been a labor of love. Most of all, I hope *The Net Worth Workout* gives you the financial peace of mind to spend the time you want with the people you love and enjoy the most.

1

THE NET WORTH
WORKOUT EXPLAINED

THE NATIONAL HEALTH AND NUTRITION EXAMINATION
SURVEY conducted between 1999 and 2002 indicates that
nearly two-thirds of U.S. citizens are overweight.[1] How can
this be? Today in the United States we have access to un-
precedented products and expertise. In every corner of the
nation, one can find low-fat foods, diet books, and a legion
of personal trainers ready to help. Chances are the gym
equipment at your local health club rivals that used by
Olympians. Still, the nation has never been in worse shape.
We all know what that means: a decreased quality of life, a
greater risk of facing a whole army of nasty diseases, and
possibly even a shortened lifespan.

Did you know that our *financial* health is just as bad? According to a survey done by researchers at the University of Michigan, a similar percentage of Americans are on shaky financial ground.[2] Few people in the history of the world have enjoyed more abundance than we do, yet as many as half of the people in the United States live paycheck to paycheck—even many with six-figure incomes.

The average U.S. citizen works 44 years, then retires with a $46,000 net worth, excluding home equity.[3] That represents just $1,000 for every year worked—$83 for every month! Those statistics tell me we're financially unfit. Meanwhile, if such a person had invested $1,000 a year in the S&P 500 for forty-four years, at age sixty-five, he would have $652,640! Ask yourself, What happened to that $600,000-plus of "missing" net worth?

Like their out-of-shape counterparts, financially unfit people don't enjoy the quality of life that they could because financial worries are forever hanging over their heads, and because their financial stamina is too poor to provide them with the lifestyle their money *could* be earning them. Just as out-of-shape people are more susceptible to disease, the financially unfit among us are at a greater risk of underfunding their retirements, not having enough to pay for their children's education, and paying high interest rates on their credit card balances. And just as extreme unfitness can shorten the life of a sedentary person, poor financial health can cause an individual's life savings to run out prematurely.

I find it tragic that so many people hit retirement with less than a year's living expenses in the bank. That's the reason I developed the Net Worth Workout: I don't want you to end up that way!

FOUR QUADRANTS OF WEALTH (FINANCIAL HEALTH)

The reasons individuals fail to achieve financial health are related to the reasons they fail to maintain good physical health. In both cases, misplaced priorities and lack of planning sabotage our well-being. When people are physically or financially unfit, it's usually because there's no *process* in place to motivate good habits

On the Net Worth Workout, you'll learn to monitor systematically four key areas of your financial health—earning, spending, saving, and investing (see Figure 1-1)—using as models four areas of *physical* health—metabolism, caloric intake, muscle strength, and cardiovascular fitness. You'll start with a realistic picture of your current status in

FIGURE 1-1. FOUR KEY AREAS OF FINANCIAL HEALTH.

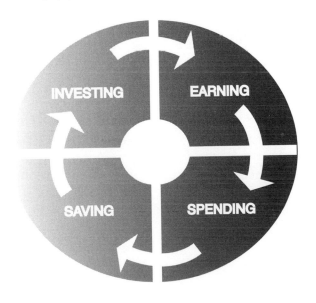

each area, set short- and long-term goals for the future, and develop doable plans for achieving these goals.

Like the body's major systems, each quadrant in Figure 1-2 has its own unique function. But also like the body's systems, the quadrants benefit from cross-training; that is, they work in synergy, each reinforcing the others. I'll show you that your personal finances form a holistic system, just like the body's physiology. In other words, any improvement to one quadrant will boost power among the others.

Earning = Metabolism

The first quadrant, *earning,* functions like your metabolism. A physically active body routes nourishment better.

FIGURE 1-2. A FINANCIAL HOLISTIC SYSTEM IS JUST LIKE THE BODY'S PHYSIOLOGY.

Quadrant = Body Sytem	Function
Earning = Metabolism:	Maximizing earnings strengthens and speeds up other quadrants.
Spending = Calorie Intake:	"Junk" spending decreases wealth; "nutritious" spending boosts it.
Saving = Strength Training:	Like weight lifting, smart saving builds "financial muscle."
Investing = Cardio Fitness:	Like cardio work, investing increases other components' capacity.

High metabolisms literally burn calories more efficiently. In fact, a triathlete like me processes food differently than a sedentary person—even if they eat exactly the same thousand-calorie meal. As an added benefit, a potent metabolism boosts your immune system, keeping you productive and vibrant. And any degree of improvement is a bonus: You needn't be in peak condition to enjoy the benefits.

The best news is that, contrary to popular opinion, our metabolisms aren't set at birth. Regular physical activity speeds the metabolism up, so we grow strong and energetic. By contrast, inactivity slows our metabolisms, so we tend to become plump and lethargic. In financial terms, your earning power, like your metabolism, depends on how well you "use" whatever you earned today and in recent weeks. By "earnings" I mean the full range of your salary and benefits. Think broadly: Earnings include any form of remuneration for your services.

Too many people believe a better job and a bigger paycheck will solve their financial worries. Naturally, you want to earn as much as possible, and from every part of your compensation package. For the time being, though, your best short-term payoff is to optimize today's paycheck and benefits package.

Like an athlete in training, it is best to acquire good habits and apply them to your existing resources. Start by asking yourself, "Have I taken the time to understand my benefits package? Am I using everything I can?" To find the answer to this question, ask yourself:

- Does my family take advantage of child or elder care that's available through work?

- Should we switch to my spouse's health plan? What deductibles and copays does my healthcare plan entail, versus its payout rates for claims? How does that compare to my spouse's options?

- Can I set up a pretax account for health-care reimbursement, commuting expenses, or child care?

Such choices can add up to big money. The Net Worth Workout shows you how to do the most with whatever you have now, so that you can carry those healthy habits with you as your paychecks grow.

Spending = Calorie Intake

The second quadrant, *spending*, is like your caloric intake; it's a nutritional issue. Just as diet can enhance your health and performance, so too spending tends to be either "good"—as protein and fiber are for the body, or a mortgage and 401(k) contribution are for a financial portfolio—or "junky"—candy bars and fast food, or trendy clothes and a pricey leased car. Whether physical or financial, maintaining and increasing fitness means recognizing these differences.

But aside from routine costs like the mortgage or the utilities bills, few people know exactly where their money goes. Granted, it can be hard to track—perhaps you don't feel you have the time to track it. The Net Worth Workout offers a process that is fast and easy. At the start, it helps you look at your fixed and variable expenses.

Equally important, we'll take a long look at your *discre-*

tionary spending. What do you want? What really rings your bell? With such realistic guidelines, you set appropriate goals and keep them in sight. Later, as your needs change over time, the program benefits you even more: You can adapt it to all kinds of changes, such as losing your job or taking care of elderly parents.

Discretionary spending is a huge quality-of-life issue. You will think about questions like:

- How important is spontancity to me? Should I make my travel plans in advance so I don't get slammed on last-minute airfares?

- Do I think of myself as generous, and what does that mean to me?

- What goods and services are truly emotionally important to me? Which ones could I do without?

The less we spend on things we don't really need or want, the more we have for things that matter. The Net Worth Workout shows you how to do that.

Saving = Strength Training

Our third quadrant, *saving*, is like strength training for building muscle: It fortifies you and gives you a means of tracking your progress. If you were planning to bike over the Rockies, you'd build strength beforehand by logging miles. But if you don't happen to live near the mountains, you'd head to the gym and focus on weight training, particularly working on your quadriceps. You'd also find a hill near your home and ride it repeatedly to gain strength.

Building financial strength by saving is no different. Saving isn't just your bank account's interest rate; it's a whole set of behaviors. It's what you put into your retirement fund, versus your employer's contribution, and what that means before and after taxes. It's what you set aside for major purchases such as furniture, vacations, or new cars. It's also about meeting long-term goals, like buying a home, funding a child's education, or retiring worry-free. It's about creating a three- to six-month "safety net" in case of a sudden short-term disability or job loss. In short, saving allows you to build financial muscle so you can "stay the course" toward a stable, satisfying future.

Investing = Cardiovascular Workout

The fourth and final quadrant, *investing*, is comparable to cardiovascular fitness. Remember, the heart powers every other part of the body. Cardio training, such as biking, running, and roller-blading, enlarges an athlete's heart and grows extra capillaries, enabling the body as a whole to do more with the same amount of effort. Likewise, as investments compound over time, the same level of effort will yield greater results.

A strong investing base functions just like your heart, providing the stamina that drives all other parts of your financial fitness program. Managed correctly over time, this income will surpass your paycheck. Such "exercise" does, of course, take time and persistence, but its returns are tremendous.

It's also important to note that sound investing relies on diversification. A good hurdler stretches and lifts weights, just as a good boxer jogs and does calisthenics. This cross-training helps the whole body perform better and lowers the risk of injury. In a similar way, diversification increases your return while reducing the risk in your portfolio. For that reason, the investing quadrant of the Net Worth Workout examines the different asset classes. You will learn how to tailor your portfolio to your goals.

Beginners can't be expected to plunge in from the high board, so first you'll dip your toes in, comparing the fundamentals of stocks and bonds. Next, you'll learn why a portfolio should include stocks from large, medium, and small companies, as well as short-, intermediate-, and long-term bonds. Finally, you'll see how it all works together.

Ultimately, the synergy of a properly executed plan creates overall fitness, keeping the body in tip-top shape. Each quadrant is fueled by the others, maximizing your total results. That's the crux of the Net Worth Workout: attaining synergy among your finances.

MAKING THE NET WORTH WORKOUT YOUR OWN

The best thing about the Net Worth Workout? You gear it to your needs, your abilities, and your resources.

Like any good trainer, I recognize that not everyone has the same capabilities or concerns. In physical terms, that means not everyone can do a hundred push-ups, nor, for that matter, would they want to. In financial terms, it means that not everyone has the same means, lifestyle, or dreams.

Step one, then, is getting to know the "financial you." What obstacles will you be facing as you move through your workout? They're different for each person.

Perhaps your paycheck "just flies out of your wallet," and you feel you should spend smarter—though, at the same time, you don't want to budget in overdrive.

Maybe you pile up statements you hardly understand, resolving to ask a loved one or savvy friend to explain them to you. Or perhaps you're embarrassed that you need to ask and therefore ask no one.

Maybe you just turned fifty and have begun to realize you don't want to spend the rest of your days punching a time clock. You know you're coming to investing for retirement a little late in the game, and you want more than anything to make the most of your last ten to fifteen years of income.

Or perhaps you'd like to be an entrepreneur. You have big dreams and are looking for a way to make them come true—without the risk of sending your family to the poorhouse. In that case, your financial portrait is all about serving both goals: making ends meet at home while seeking start-up funds for your dream.

Once you have a clear picture of your financial priorities, you'll know what kinds of goals to set. In almost every case, it starts with a certain amount of training to gain the basics of "how to." What high school coach would send a team against rivals unprepared? It's the same for us distance runners: No sane marathoner comes to the starting line without completing enough long runs. Success in finance is more about perspiration than inspiration. You have to build a "workout" into your lifestyle. That's where you reap benefits.

For most of us, the problem isn't finding the resources; it's finding the time and energy, and having a system to sort through this array of choices. We feel overloaded with information; it paralyzes us into inaction and apathy. Sometimes it's overwhelming and we opt to do nothing.

What makes the similarity between physical and financial health so striking—and relevant—is that in both cases it has little to do with external factors, like having the best shoes and perfect weather to train in, getting the right interest rate, or knowing the perfect mutual fund to invest in.

First and foremost, winning happens within. Start by believing in yourself; most of the rest, you'll find, boils down to training and conditioning.

The right training is vital, especially for rookies. It's not enough to be familiar with the rules or to follow the play-by-play. You have to practice, drill, and *internalize* the moves. That's how you make progress, how you "get into the game."

If only more people understood this dynamic! Without this training, most people revert to old habits after a brief infatuation with "getting into shape." It's no wonder that the typical American arrives at retirement with only $44,000!

The good news, though, is that behavioral scientists have developed techniques to beat our inertia. Apparently, we all share a natural resistance to maintaining and improving our health, both physical and financial. Yet behavioral economists now know that the methods that help people get and stay physically fit work equally well at getting us financially fit. Better yet, neither process takes hours a week or requires suffering. You can build your net worth and feel better about your money using the financial means you already have.

To achieve both physical and financial fitness, you must make sure you prepare adequately:

1. Start by consulting an expert, whether a personal trainer or financial adviser.

2. Set specific goals, whether it is running a marathon or retiring at sixty.

3. Use the right equipment, such as a good pair of running shoes or a solid portfolio of mutual funds.

4. Practice regularly, whether getting in your daily run or monitoring your investments.

5. Accept setbacks, which may range from being injured to losing some money in the market.

The Net Worth Workout is designed to help you structure your way through each of these tips.

This book will help you tap into cutting-edge theory from the world's leading behavioral economists, as well as learn from my experience counseling thousands of clients just like you. It draws, too, on my years in competitive sports, which taught me the link between vision, persistence, and success.

As you begin setting specific goals, the Net Worth Workout will show you the mechanics of achieving the goals you set. As a financial adviser, one of the first things I teach clients is the "one-two": Articulate your goals, then draft a detailed, realistic plan to reach them. What amazes me is that regardless of whether a person's financial goal has five or eight figures, the process is essentially the same.

Next, you must choose the right equipment to achieve your goals. Throughout this book, I'll discuss the financial products that are available to help you achieve your goals, from CDs and money market accounts to 401(k)s and other tax-advantaged accounts. You'll understand each of these products in terms of what they'll do for your financial fitness.

Practicing regularly involves making your financial health a high enough priority to incorporate it into your daily life. This is where it's good to know you're not alone. Several times a week, I meet up with my triathlon-training pals. We discuss which races we want to do, the times we hope to achieve in them, and how much training they'll require. We compare personal experiences, and then develop a program for the season. Each of us has come up with a training schedule that, depending on our professional and personal schedules, adjusts as the season progresses.

By doing this together, we have more fun and get better results than going solo. I find the same sense of empowerment among my clients anytime we forge a partnership.

Finally, you must learn to accept setbacks, because that will help you to continue to have the willpower to keep moving forward, even if you have to stop and recalibrate your plan. Many people give up on their diet-and-exercise regimens the first time they step on the scale and discover that they've gained a half pound. Everyone experiences setbacks: Athletes get injured, investments don't pan out, and unexpected expenses arise. But you won't be tempted to give up when setbacks come along, because we'll develop a plan for handling them before they can sabotage your goals. You'll learn to balance your portfolio (your diet and exercise regimen) and reserve enough cash (downtime) to avoid injury and pain. Even when setbacks occur, you'll know how to deal with them so they won't cause devastation.

WHAT TO EXPECT ON THE NET WORTH WORKOUT

Now that you have a general understanding of the purpose of the Net Worth Workout, let's take a look at what you'll be doing throughout the rest of the book.

Chapter Two is about attitude; it's the pep talk you need to get started. You'll learn why you're as capable of success as anyone else. I'll help you visualize that success, showing how to break through your barriers and how your mind-set can bring you results. I've put this attitude adjustment first, even before we do a thorough evaluation of your current financial fitness level, because it is essential to your success in this program that you approach it from a winning mind-set.

Chapter Three is a thorough examination of your financial health—your shape, goals, and plan. First we'll assess your current financial situation using the Health/Wealth Test. A kind of "body mass index" for finances, this test helps you get a full, accurate picture of your overall financial condition.

Next we talk about your goals. Just as you would determine how many pounds you needed to lose to get in shape, or how much speed and stamina you needed to gain for a particular athletic event, you'll now need to identify your financial goals. I'll walk you through the process of establishing reasonable and achievable financial aims, taking into account your personal interests and concerns. These goals include short-term ones, such as setting up an emergency reserve or caring for an aging parent, and long-term ones, like buying a home or ensuring a comfortable retirement.

Once you're introduced to the program, I'll help you "get with the program" by implementing it. We'll divide the goals you outlined in Chapter Three into the four quadrants of earning, spending, saving, and investing. Together, we'll move through a series of exercises to determine what's most important to you in each quadrant. After we review your total assets and liabilities, you'll set clear, reasonable goals for each quadrant.

Chapters Four through Seven cover one quadrant apiece. Through a variety of specially designed exercises, each chapter prompts you to develop a detailed, in-depth picture of your present condition. The chapters also include real-life examples of changes you can make to build your net worth.

Finally, Chapter Eight shows how to "get it all together" and coordinate your efforts in all four quadrants, acquiring habits for lasting prosperity.

Now that we've covered the basics of the Net Worth Workout, you're ready to take the first step toward achieving your financial potential. Let's get started!

NOTES

1. National Health and Nutrition Examination Survey (NHANES), 1999–2002, (Atlanta: Centers for Disease Control and Prevention); available at http://www.cdc.gov/nchs/data/nhanes/databriefs/adultweight.pdf.

2. Elena Gouskova and Frank Stafford, "Trends in Household Wealth Dynamics, 1999–2001" (Institute for Social Research, University of Michigan, September 2002), p. 3. http://psidonline.isr.umich.edu/Publications/Papers/TrendsIndynamics1999-2001.pdf.

3. Annamaria Lusardi, "Explaining Why So Many People Do Not Save," (Center for Retirement Research, Boston College, September 2001, p. 35). www.bc.edu/centers/crr/papers/wp_2001-05.pdf.

ATTITUDE

WHAT'S THE KEY INGREDIENT in any successful financial plan?

It's not your income level, your organizational skills, or even your financial savvy.

It's your attitude.

Over time, a persistent, winning attitude will help you capitalize on your strengths, overcome your shortcomings, and marshal all the other assets you need to succeed. By contrast, a defeatist attitude can waste away even the highest income.

And, as this chapter will show, your financial attitude is a matter of choice.

Granted, money is an emotional topic. Once people realize what they've been missing, they tend to judge themselves too harshly. But whatever your financial holdings, you already have strengths that can serve you well. Even bad habits often can be used to advantage. For instance, if you spend too freely, I know you're not intimidated by money. This quality will come in handy when deciding on investments. Besides, whatever your strengths, the Net Worth Workout will build on them, adding new skills to give you the tools a successful investor needs.

To help you along, I have to be a good trainer—which means earning your trust.

In my years as a financial adviser, I've found that negative emotions are the main reason people delay taking action to fix their finances. Money fears prevent us from pursuing the life we truly want. Many of my clients also avoid making changes to their financial situation because they are fearful they could end up worse off rather than more secure.

Maybe you associate saving with scrimping, like in that first year after college. Was it a treat to eat canned tuna on payday? Did you drive to the far end of town once a week to save a few quarters on gas? Or maybe you feel guilty when you think about retiring, since Dad never had that option.

Perhaps, like many of us, you simply consider all investments "too risky." That tells me two things: I need to teach you about your investment options, and I need to show you the risks of *not* investing. If your fear of risk drives you to stash all your money in a savings account, each year you'll keep less of your *current* earnings than people making the same income who invest their savings. In a typical savings account you earn about the same rate as inflation, 3.8 percent, while a typical investment in long-term government bonds has averaged 5.3 percent. The S&P 500 averages about 10 percent, though it has much more risk than savings accounts or government bonds. You can see how using instruments to fight inflation and maximize tax breaks helps you to prepare for the future.

Without these kinds of investments, you're like a marathoner who is going to compete in high-altitude Colorado yet continues to train at low altitudes. You're handicapping yourself.

So if you are risk-averse, it's time to recognize the real risk is in *taking no risks*.

INCREASE YOUR FINANCIAL INTELLIGENCE

Just by reading this book, you're already accomplishing one of the most important steps in becoming financially fit: You're increasing your level of awareness of how you think about your finances. According to Annamaria Lusardi, an economics professor at Dartmouth College, that step alone can add significantly to your bottom line.

Lusardi has shown that offering workers seminars on financial planning and retirement topics significantly increases their wealth. Such programs, according to the study, can increase employees' wealth by 15 percent to 20 percent—regardless of their respective income levels.

Raising your level of financial intelligence is the beginning of real progress. Just like with physical fitness, once you bring the subject into your active consciousness and become realistic about what you're capable of, you begin making active choices toward improvement right away. For instance, if you've decided to lose ten pounds to look great for your college reunion, you might take that extra flight of stairs instead of the elevator or order diet instead of regular Coke.

Best of all, as you make it a habit to remain conscious of your financial life, similarly modest behavioral changes can work miracles over time. In Chapter Seven on investing, for instance, you'll see what a difference it makes to put 10 percent instead of 5 percent of your salary into your 401(k), or to start contributing $4,000 yearly to a Roth IRA.

Once you begin to put your new financial intelligence into action, you'll start seeing new possibilities and forming new routines. The tiny change you make today pays you back with less stress right from the beginning, and as conscious changes today become the unconscious habits of tomorrow, you'll generate long-term wealth in the future.

Ask any finance expert: Prosperity needn't be a function of your income. In fact, people with similar incomes can have dramatically different net worth. Rather, wealth is a function of how informed you are and how willing you are to improve your situation.

Building a healthy financial attitude, then, is a two-step process. Step one: Become aware of your financial circumstances. Step two: Make it a high priority to *keep* yourself aware.

"BUT I DON'T HAVE TIME TO THINK ABOUT FINANCES!"

When I sit down with a new client, I start by asking two key questions: Have you tried assessing your future recently? And, what aspects of your finances hold you back?

Among those people who've put off financial matters, the reason I hear most often is "not enough time." A study of financial planning behaviors published in *The Millionaire Next Door* came to the same conclusion. People cite lack of time as the primary reason they haven't planned their investments. Variations of this response are:

"I know nothing about investments, and it would take too much time to learn."

"I'd love to take a class, but I just don't have the time."

If, instead of discussing financial planning, we were talking about exercise, would the responses be much different? How about eating healthier? It probably doesn't surprise you that year after year, America's top-three New Year's resolutions are "losing weight," "getting in shape," and "handling money better." No wonder 68 percent of fiscally unfit Americans plan to get their finances in shape "as soon as I find the time."

FIND THE TIME TO HANDLE YOUR MONEY

If there's one attitude that contributes the most to financial success, it's the Western view of time. In our culture we say "Time is money" and "*Carpe diem,*" but few of us grasp the full impact of compounded interest—what we call "the time value of money." Once you know how colossal a financial opportunity time can be, your priorities will change, and you'll *make sure* you have the time to manage your finances effectively.

To do that, you have to start planning.

To get a fitness workout in, don't you usually have to plan a time? Most of the people I know need that kind of structure. Getting the workout onto your schedule helps make it happen.

Reinventing your financial health takes similar behaviors. According to *The Millionaire Next Door,* most people who are adept at creating wealth agree with the following statements: "I spend a lot of time planning my financial future," and "Usually I have sufficient time to handle my investments properly." That's what I call the right attitude! By contrast, people who accumulate less wealth agree with these statements: "I can't devote enough time to my investment decisions," and "I'm just too busy to spend much time with my own financial affairs."[1]

Even early in our first conversation, I can spot the clients who've made "finding time" a priority. They're usually well prepared, often arriving with spreadsheets of their holdings. Take Bob and Maureen. When they first came in to see me, they said that every year they faithfully set aside a weekend to thoroughly review their financial situation. I was very impressed. How could I contribute to their productivity? Along with advising them on certain choices, I helped them consolidate their accounts. Now, the time they used to spend gathering statements is used to help them understand their investments.

Everyone, of course, knows about the time-money bind. But what I find shocking is how close lower-performing investors come to success, in terms of the time they commit. In *The Millionaire Mind,* Thomas J. Stanley interviewed people about their habits. Those who agreed with the statement, "I have sufficient time to handle my investments," spent an average of 8.4 hours per month on their finances, and they prospered over time. Yet those who agreed with the statement, "I never have the time to make it pay off," logged a respectable 4.6 hours a month![2]

In other words, that extra hour a week (or seven-plus minutes a day) can make all the difference. If we set our minds to it, most of us could spare another hour a week. Financial security is not hard to attain when you put in the time.

UNDERSTAND OPPORTUNITY COST

Every choice, even the smallest one, has a cost involved. There is often a financial cost, but there is also the cost of time spent, and the cost of not being able to do one thing because you are doing something else. Thus, assessing a course of action involves identifying the opportunity costs—the time, the money, and so on—of choosing one course over all possible courses. All kinds of decisions have opportunity costs. For instance, to figure the opportunity cost of a road race you want to enter, you'd probably consider its duration, level of difficulty, and location. You could enter a long race two states away and be gone for an entire weekend, or you could sign up for a shorter local race and spend the rest of your weekend at your daughter's soccer game and relaxing with your family. The race two states away may have a lower entry fee, but you would also have to consider other costs, such as paying for gas, staying in a hotel, buying food, even the cost of driving for several hours. These costs may all be worth it because you'll try something new, see friends you haven't seen in a few months, and have a chance to get away. You have to decide if the costs are worth it.

Analyzing your financial decisions, *even small ones,* in terms of their opportunity cost is a powerful way to improve your financial shape.

With money, especially smaller sums, we're tempted to be cavalier, as if every dollar held equal significance. Just as no calorie is "just a calorie," no dollar is "just a dollar." But over the long haul, aggregated into thousands of choices, the financial implications loom large indeed.

We make these small decisions every day with our money and with our time. People who have built wealth have done it on an even grander scale: They've made a decision to spend another eight hours a month planning finances, rather than watching television, talking on the phone, or, perhaps, working.

In the space below, write five things you've done lately and the opportunity cost associated with it:

ACTIVITY	BENEFIT	OPPORTUNITY COST
1. _____	_____	_____
2. _____	_____	_____
3. _____	_____	_____
4. _____	_____	_____
5. _____	_____	_____

Your grandparents understood opportunity cost; chances are your parents mastered it, too. Both groups grew up believing in the adage, "Look after the pennies, and the dollars will look after themselves." The idea is to limit small purchases so that you can handle big ones when needed. It's a great formula for success.

That isn't to say that you should simply squirrel away all your money. There's an enormous opportunity cost in doing that. Once you start to accrue "real money," put it to work. Consider the following cautionary tale.

For two years, Gerald kept most of his money in cash, though I explained the importance of diversifying. We discussed his goals and his tolerance for risk. Gradually, he came to accept that leaving his funds in a savings account, safe but fully taxed, was accruing too great an opportunity cost. Finally, he took the plunge and invested some money. By the following year, his account had grown very nicely. Gerald saw slow, steady growth in addition to certain tax benefits. So what was the problem? He'd invested only 10 percent of his cash! Sure, he grew $5,000 into $5,400 tax-free, but the $50,000 in his savings account grew to only $51,500—and that $1,500 in earnings was taxed. Had Gerald considered the opportunity cost of keeping so much money in a savings account and instead invested all of this money, his earnings likely would have been $59,400, perhaps even tax-free!

I'm sorry to say this kind of thing happens all the time, to people all over the country. Not long ago, a very sharp lawyer, Carol, came to see me. She kept $40,000 in her bank account. It was earning 2 percent. She confided to me that she had a number of similar accounts in various banks. That practice is fairly common. Many people feel safer sprinkling their assets around. But Carol, like Gerald, was not building the wealth she could have been had she been considering the opportunity cost of her actions.

What's surprising is that Carol had sought help on the same issue four years earlier—and she had heard exactly the same advice. So the opportunity cost of her actions impacted her today and over the last four years. I had recommended that she keep some money in savings, diversify her assets (particularly with tax-free bonds), and so on. Now, her situation has changed: Carol works part-time so that she can care for her three-year-old daughter. She could have been earning tax-free income from her investments. She also could have started a college savings plan for her daughter. It's more important than ever that her money work hard for her so that she can have peace of mind.

Compare Carol's case to a person who has made a commitment to get in shape. Usually, after much planning and discussion with a trainer, the person sweats through the first workout, then gets into a regular routine and begins to see results. But what if our would-be hard-body showed up at the gym for a one-hour consultation with a trainer, then disappeared for six months? Would that one-hour session have helped him get in shape? It may be an extreme example, but you know it happens. People have very good intentions to do their workouts religiously, but then keep putting them off.

Now that you're resolved to change your future, you'll derive the greatest benefit from committing to it for the long haul. And that means making it a habit to weigh the opportunity cost of each financial decision that you make—including those you make "by default."

THE TWO-HOUR MILLIONAIRE'S WORKOUT

The Net Worth Workout offers several key exercises to stretch your capabilities. Here's the first! Care to work out like a millionaire? This week, commit to spending two hours improving your finances, and earmark the same two hours each week through the end of the month. Go ahead—schedule it in now. (Of course, you're already spending time, reading this book, but we'll overlook that for now.)

Can't possibly come up with two spare hours a week

right now? Okay, let's make it one hour for starters. But plan on adding ten minutes a month to your weekly "financial hour" until you've built all the way up to two hours, because there's magic in that second hour, as I'll explain in a moment.

What should you do with your time? The specifics of each session are up to you. Don't worry, though; I will be giving plenty of suggestions throughout the book! But for now, think in terms of organization and education: that is, getting all aspects of your financial life in order, one at a time, and gaining new knowledge about financial tools and concepts that can help you in the future. Here are some of the tasks you might tackle during your session:

- Organize your bank statements.

- Check the performance of your retirement accounts.

- Learn what a Roth IRA is.

- Call your bank and ask about a program to accelerate your mortgage payments.

Whatever you do, use a timer, because the point is to pace yourself and *just* spend the time you've assigned.

The second part of this assignment: After you've finished your financial organization and education session, ask yourself four questions:

1. How do you feel?

_____

_____

_____

2. Do you feel more in control of your money? Why is that?

_____

_____

_____

3. Are you glad you took the time to think about your finances? How have you benefited?

_____

_____

_____

4. What would you rather do differently?

_____

_____

_____

Now, stop and consider the most important question. Do you think that spending an additional hour a week on your finances would deprive you of anything truly important? Would you miss out on something that could have changed your life?

What *can* change your life is taking charge of your finances and embarking on a new destiny. Ultimately, financial security *frees up* your time, giving you new choices about where and with whom to spend it. To me, that's time well spent.

GO FOR THE "FLOW"

If you start with an hour a week, I want you to commit yourself to building up to two hours as quickly as you can, because that second hour is crucial. For millionaires, that extra weekly hour brings them to a learning threshold. It seems that thinking about your finances for over eight hours a month helps you internalize certain key principles. Some people would call this quantum leap in understanding "being in the flow state." Ultimately, "flow" gives millionaires more financial security.

What, exactly, is flow? And how do you get it? The term was coined by Mihaly Csikszentmihalyi, a University of Chicago professor of psychology and education. Flow refers to those times in your life when your concentration is so strong that you're totally absorbed in the activity. You feel alert, in effortless control, and at the peak of your abilities.

It's the state of mind elite athletes constantly strive for. But athletes just don't break into flow from the moment they suit up; it's a process, a skill acquired over time. Virtually every flow-producing activity requires your attention before it becomes enjoyable. Think of this up-front commitment as "activation energy"; you need it to enjoy any complex activity.

If you work out, you know exactly what I mean. In a standard session, most of us find the first quarter-hour unpleasant. Our bodies may resist; it takes getting used to. But once we do adjust, we start feeling much better.

Like athletes, people who create wealth go through this cycle over and over again. Millionaires consistently take the time each month to *plan* their investments (which means more than just going online and seeing what the total of their portfolio is); it's part of their practice. They work through the uncomfortable part because they're going for the flow. What they're doing, meanwhile, is building emotional strength and resiliency. Let me give you an example.

Last week a young woman named Jill, who works in marketing for a large financial institution, came to me to talk about her financial situation. Her company had announced cutbacks and she was taking a severance package after working there for five years. Jill had about $60,000 in her 401(k). I congratulated her for being so disciplined about her savings—she was just thirty-four years old. But Jill had withdrawn $15,000 from another 401(k), closing it out when she was twenty-seven to travel through Europe.

When I recommended that she put less of her 401(k) in the stable value fund—a fixed account earning 4 percent—and more in international, small companies and high-yield bonds, I saw her flinch. She had lost a lot in the bear market of 2000 and was letting fear determine how she invested. I showed her that by diversifying her 401(k) she could earn a higher return over the next thirty years. If she stayed in a fixed account and inflation averaged 3 percent, then her money wouldn't be doing anything more than keeping even with inflation.

And that $15,000 of 401(k) money she spent on a trip to Europe? If she had left it in the 401(k) and it grew at 10 percent, she could have over $443,000 by the time she was sixty-five. A very expensive trip indeed!

The more we studied her retirement account as it might look in various scenarios, the more confidence she gained. Of course, she wanted to make the most of her $60,000. I also pointed out that if she worked until she was sixty-five, at her current savings rate, she would contribute at least another $465,000 to her 401(k). That changed her perspective from being overly cautious with this $60,000 to realizing she had time to let money grow since she'd be adding money every year for thirty years. Once she really got into the flow, she was able to drop her fears and invest in a manner that was more age-appropriate. She began to embrace being uncomfortable today to be financially comfortable much later.

In order to achieve flow, we must be willing to work through the initial stress. Stress is what makes every athlete perform better. Just as our muscles require stress to develop and grow, so do our financial attitudes. Cutting ourselves off from stress can make us apathetic, and hurt us in the long run. Unless we confront stress regularly, we lose our capacity for coping with it.

So when you sit down to work on your finances, and you spend the first fifteen minutes wanting to throw your calculator at a wall, hang in there. Work it. You're on your way to flow.

Sure, just getting organized to tackle your finances takes time. It takes most people ten to fifteen minutes just to get organized and start, and the same to finish up. Here are some examples of the little "housekeeping" tasks people face:

- Where'd I put the password for my retirement account?

- I need to go online and check my deductible for the health-care account; what happened to that statement?

■ Have I filed that health-care claim yet?

■ Who took the calculator?

Streamline the time it takes to start working toward flow by being aware of the way you spend it. What activities eat into your financial planning time? Your next exercise is to list where you think you waste the most time. Here's a hint: Imagine that you're an efficiency expert watching a recording of yourself in your home office, or wherever that activity occurs. How's your paperwork? Can you find things easily? Is your workspace free of clutter—and interruptions?

Make a list of whatever you'd like to modify, and write next to each item any emotions that surface in this process. For example, "Frustration: playroom too close and noisy," "Confusion: this prospectus might just as well be written in Swahili," and so forth. Make it a part of your session to deal with at least one of these frustrations each time you sit down to work on your finances. As you do so, you're gradually expanding the time you can spend in flow.

How I Spend My Financial Planning Time

Time-Wasters

1. _____

2. _____

3. _____

Things I Would Like to Change

The Problem		Why It's a Problem
1.		
2.		
3.		

PROSPERITY IS A PROCESS

We all want quick fixes. We'd rather do something once and call it done than commit to something long term with gradual results. So when we learn that we have to commit to a process, instead of performing a single task, we procrastinate and do nothing. But with finance—just as with fitness—there's really no other choice: Coasting always takes us in a downward spiral.

Perhaps you hoped to have all the answers by the end of this book; that this program would somehow zap away all your financial worries. I'm here to tell you that no financial adviser should promise that. Though I want you to be satisfied that you're doing the right thing, a quick fix is never in your best interest. You're much better off staying open to the possibilities that each month and year offers.

That means that you can't entirely relax—ever. Perhaps it's a vestige of the survival instinct, but even financial pros get a bit edgy when we think about our holdings. It's inevitable: Money is linked on every level to your life experience, which is always in flux.

Ultimately, you need to call the shots: You know what works for you, and what doesn't, far better than I ever could. Besides, your anxiety is always less when you're in charge.

Remember that, just like your body, your financial holdings are constantly influenced by external factors. What's up in your personal life? Our priorities change, sometimes even month-to-month. Who hasn't struggled with their weight when they switched to a desk job, or run up the balance on a credit card during the holidays? Then come the outside factors, like the economy: How's your job security? Is now the time to jump ship and start that new business? Maybe you're thinking of selling the house. Or maybe you should take out a home equity loan and renovate so you don't have to buy a bigger home.

By all means, when facing such questions, seek financial advice. As your coach, I want you to learn what feels right for you, what you're ready for. As you reach interim goals, you'll reframe what you can achieve, thereby gaining confidence. And when fate rules against you, you'll have tools to overcome that adversity—and to minimize the odds of recurrence. In the final analysis, you're in charge.

If there's one message in this chapter, it's this: Managing money is as an ongoing "self-improvement" project. The Net Worth Workout teaches financial management as a *process*—not as an end. Prosperity is a horizon to sail toward, not a pedestal to stand upon. There may be a change in the winds in your course, but that keeps the excitement in your journey.

We also need to defy the myth that other people don't

struggle with their finances. Everyone does sometimes. Like primo athletes, even the very wealthy can't deliver a perfect performance every time. Consider Babe Ruth, the first man to strike out a thousand times. He just didn't let it stop him; it's how he became one of the greatest hitters of all time.

Yes, successful investors make their share of mistakes. Nobody has constantly perfect information. Every Richie Rich or the self-made billionaire has bungled something along the way. Donald Trump springs to mind, but we've also had Thomas Edison, Henry Ford, and thousands of others since. While developing the nickel/iron storage battery, Edison performed 10,295 failed experiments. Michael Jordan was cut from his high school basketball team. And Colonel Sanders, needing income, tried to sell his cherished family recipe for fried chicken. It was turned down by more than 1,000 restaurants before he started Kentucky Fried Chicken.

Those who create wealth choose their good habits. Certain forms of discipline—typically small actions and incremental adjustments—become a part of their lives. Self-made successes keep their eyes on the prize and "automate" decisions as often as possible. (For instance, payroll deductions amass savings while shielding us from temptation.) Best of all, people who are successful with their money not only set goals; they reach most of them.

And they reach them by staying committed to the process.

The only way you're going to make progress is to commit. Don't overthink it. Follow the exercises in this book, speak with an adviser, and get into the game. Otherwise you could succumb to what we financial advisers call "analysis paralysis."

Analysis paralysis is one end of the spectrum; the other end is flying blind. Sometimes people just coast along, fearing to ask questions and learn what they've been missing. And it's especially hard to change your habits when you conclude "there's never enough time," or that you've never been good with money. This defeatist attitude is the most dangerous because it leaves you vulnerable to all kinds of irrational behaviors.

Train yourself to take the time that's necessary to make intelligent, informed choices.

CHANGE SHOULD HAPPEN SLOWLY

Remember, change should be gradual. It can't "stick" if you tackle ten things at once. One of the most common mistakes people make is trying to change all their negative behaviors too quickly. Most of us feel that change "just takes sheer willpower." That's not true. It's important to keep your expectations realistic and manageable. Otherwise, when day-to-day issues return to the forefront of our awareness, we slip up on our overly ambitious goals. Then, the next thing we know, we've given up. (Consider that most New Year's resolutions have petered out by the end of January.)

You know, the emotional baggage may be the worst part. We're left feeling that we've failed—guilty instead of optimistic. Then we put the project off, only to try it again the next season, year, or decade.

One reason why most of us fail is because we make the goal too precise, without specifying how it is going to be reached. A weight-control plan offers a good parallel. For instance, rather than focusing on how much you're going to lose, you're better off focusing on the things you can control: how many times you'll get to that low-impact aerobic class, or how many times you'll meet with your personal trainer each week, or how often you'll have dessert. After all, today is the only day you have control over.

You need to treat your finances the same way. You can learn what you're spending, how to contribute to a college-savings plan, and so on. Just take it incrementally. Remember, the Net Worth Workout is always a process, never an event. You do what feels right for you, what's achievable, what you're ready for.

FIGHT TALK: YOU'RE ALREADY A CHAMP

Trust me, you have the ability to prosper. You're just as capable as anyone.

I meet hotshots with no inkling of what prosperity requires, and humble souls who've grown big accounts. The key is learning what to do. And you already know how to achieve a worthwhile goal.

Consider what you've accomplished in other areas of your life: Have you raised a family, cared for an ailing parent, held office, or completed an advanced degree? Did you travel overseas in the military, work your way through school, or attain mastery in a demanding hobby? You already know the process. Building wealth is no different.

You know that every new endeavor begins with an awkward phase. Do you remember being a child and learning to descend stairs—or have you watched a child do it lately? It's a very clumsy, uncertain process, even more complex than learning to walk. Yet ever since you were small, your physique has managed staircases.

Or perhaps you compete in athletic events. When you started, were you certain of success? Did it matter, after all, once you "got it in gear"?

On a fundamental level, you achieved every one of your accomplishments because you had faith in yourself. It may have been just a little faith, but even that can open the door to new behaviors. You can do this.

Now that your attitude is focused, it's time to start shaping your financial workout. In the next chapter, you'll examine your current shape and personal goals. You'll weigh the trade-offs, the implications of waiting versus acting today, and you'll begin to look at the steps involved in the process.

Let's make it happen!

NOTES

1. Thomas J. Stanley and William D. Danko, *The Millionaire Next Door*. (Marietta, GA: Longstreet Press, 1996), p. 96.

2. Thomas J. Stanley, *The Millionaire Mind*. (Kansas City: Andrews McMeel Publishing, 2000), p. 97.

YOUR SHAPE, GOALS, AND PLANS

IF YOU WERE STARTING a serious exercise regimen, you'd first go to your doctor for a physical checkup. Let's begin your new financial regimen the same way.

Consider this chapter your "financial checkup." I'll help you conduct a thorough evaluation of your financial condition by looking at three basic elements of the Net Worth Workout:

- Your *shape*, meaning your current financial state

- Your *goals*, meaning the financial aspects of the things you intend to achieve in the future

■ Your *plans,* which are the step-by-step "road maps" you create to take you to your goals

Together, we'll work out exactly where you are now, where you want to go, and what you must do to get there.

YOUR SHAPE

What shape are you in at this moment? What is your current financial condition? If you're going to get from point A to point B, we must start by defining point A. When starting a new fitness program, your doctor assesses your fitness level. The process usually involves weighing you, taking your blood pressure, checking your heart rate, and finding your body mass index. To assess your financial fitness level, I'll put you through a similar checkup: the Net Worth Statement, a kind of "weigh in and body mass index" for finances. The Net Worth Statement will give you an accurate picture of your overall financial condition.

If you're like many of my clients, when you complete your Net Worth Statement, you'll start feeling better right away—even if you initially thought of it as a punishment. You may even discover you have more assets than you thought.

This exercise is not meant to frighten or embarrass you by pointing out how far behind you are. It's a necessary starting point in the process that leads to better financial health. Even if the thought of taking a long, hard look at your finances scares you—the way stepping on a scale scares some people—do it anyway, and praise yourself for being courageous. It's only by an ongoing commitment to reality that we can get healthier.

Have you ever watched a large marathon, like the ones they run in New York City and Boston? It's a virtual human parade. In the front are the elite runners, 125 pounds of pure muscle, blazing along at five minutes per mile. But keep watching and the scenery will change. After the super-athletes come the weekend warriors and, finally, a group of runners who seem to do little more than shuffle along. You'll notice the spectators cheer wildly for everyone, be-cause all the runners are working so hard. Every one of these runners began the race at the same place and time, with the same fundamental goal, to complete a 26.2-mile course.

The difference is that some came to the starting line in better shape.

The better your financial shape at the beginning, the better prepared you will be to meet your goals. Together, you and I will be able to work on a number of things right off the bat to improve the shape you are in at the starting line. But we can't start working on your financial condition until we know what we're starting with.

This step is critical because the point of the workout is to get your net worth to grow as effortlessly as possible. Besides, finding out where you stand right now will help you feel much better about what you have done so far.

The Net Worth Statement will give you the most accu-rate picture of where you stand, as far as your assets and liabilities are concerned.

Using the physical fitness analogy, think of your assets as the benchmarks you've already achieved: *I've lost eight pounds; I can run a mile nonstop.* In terms of financial fitness, assets are what you've already accumulated, what you already have working for you. They typically fall into two categories: liquid and nonliquid. Liquid assets are savings accounts, insured money market accounts (IMMAs), stocks, bonds, mutual funds, CDs, cash-value life insurance, and similar items that can be readily converted to cash. Nonliquid assets are your home, other real estate, jewelry, cars, and furniture—items that are more difficult to convert to cash.

It is important to distinguish between appreciating and depreciating assets. A home appreciates; a car depreciates. This is a significant distinction: The typical home appreciates by about 5 percent a year; the typical new car loses half its value when you drive it off the lot!

Liabilities, in our health metaphor, are like the twelve pounds you have yet to lose, or the muscle strength you lost when you took six months off your weight-training routine. Liabilities can help things appreciate or depreciate, depending on whether the item for which the debt was incurred gains or loses value over time. A mortgage is the most common liability, but you may also have home equity loans, student loans (education typically appreciates because it pays for itself—and then some), credit cards, car loans (cars typically depreciate), and other debts.

It's time to add it all up. Pull out your statements, or go online and print them out. Track down the most recent appraisal of your home's value. Use an online automotive value calculator like Edmunds.com or Kelley Blue Book to figure your car's worth. Round the numbers to the nearest hundred just to make it easier.

Which statements should you use? The first time you do this exercise, I recommend that you base your figures on year-end numbers, particularly if it's early in the year. For instance, if it's February, use last December's statements. Thereafter, you can go to the most recent quarter: June or September, for instance.

I want to encourage you to set up your Net Worth Statement so that you can monitor it quarterly and track your improvements. One reason people don't do better with their finances is that they only look at the "big picture" annually, if at all. Once they get their April taxes filed, it's out of sight, out of mind until next year's tax season. But if you monitor your financial health quarterly, you can spot your weaknesses quickly and adjust. One of the secrets of becoming financially fit is staying on top of your situation. After all, if you only stepped on the bathroom scale once a year, how would you know if your dieting efforts were paying off?

A word to the wise: As long as you're getting all the information together, take the time to get everything organized. You'll thank yourself for it the next time you sit down for one of your "financial sessions."

Now, use the information on your documents to fill in the chart shown in Figure 3-1. Use this chart as a guide— you may have more or different assets and liabilities than the ones I've listed.

Next to each asset, write its value in dollars. Next to

FIGURE 3-1.
YOUR NET WORTH STATEMENT.

Assets	Value	Rate	Liabilities	Balance	Rate
Home:	_____	_____	Mortgage:	_____	_____
Savings/CDs/IMMA:	_____	_____	Home Equity:	_____	_____
401(k)/Profit Sharing:	_____	_____	Car Loan:	_____	_____
Pension:	_____	_____	Credit Cards:	_____	_____
IRAs:	_____	_____	Student Loans:	_____	_____
Stocks/Bonds:	_____	_____	401(k) Loan:	_____	_____
Cash-Value Life Insurance:	_____	_____			

TOTAL ASSETS: _____ TOTAL LIABILITIES: _____

each liability, write the amount you owe. Once you have tallied these numbers, we need to know how productively these assets and liabilities are working for you. To the right of the assets column, you'll find a column to insert the rate you're earning on your asset. For instance, your CD may be earning 3 percent. To the right of the liabilities column, insert the rate of interest you're paying on your liabilities. Here's where many of us take a deep breath—and a leap of faith. Once you've filled in all the numbers, total all your assets. Next, total all your liabilities. Then subtract liabilities from assets ("assets minus liabilities"). This number is your current total net worth—the body mass index number for your finances.

By now you're probably asking, "So, am I normal? What should my net worth be for my age and income level?" If you're looking for an indicator of average net worth, such calculations do exist. But I don't use them because I've never found them to be very helpful. Our goal is to improve your net worth, whatever it is to begin with.

A high school teacher of mine was fond of saying, "Comparison is odious." Instead of comparing yourself to some kind of national average, which can't help but be a somewhat arbitrary number, use the figure you've come up with only to compare where you are today to where you plan to be in the future. Those are the only numbers that are truly meaningful.

Let's say you're a basketball fan. You want your team to make it to the conference finals. But if they're down two games at this point, you know they'll have to work that much harder to reach the championship.

That's what these numbers will tell you: the amount of work that you'll have to do to make it to your own personal championship. I see people do it all the time—and many of them have started in real predicaments. The good news is that even if you don't "make the finals," you'll wind up in much better standing than you would otherwise.

If your Net Worth Statement reveals some nasty surprises, don't despair. We can do a number of things right now to get you to the starting line in better shape, simply by adopting new practices that provide better leverage for your opportunities. Virtually everyone I've worked with has been pleasantly surprised by the potential for improvement, once they understand the stakes and eventual payoffs. Remember, this exercise is about improving your financial lifestyle, which is a process, not an event.

Are you making payments on a high-interest credit card? You can pay off that debt with a home equity line of credit that will earn you a tax break. If you're like the typical American, you may be surprised to see how many credit cards are on your Net Worth Statement. The national average is seven cards, with balances totaling more than $8,000 across all cards. On the other hand, if you consolidate your credit card debt, opting to pay for purchases using your debit card and lowest-rate credit card, you can cut up your cards for department stores and gas stations. Doing this should lower your monthly payments and interest rates, not to mention freeing up your time: You'll have fewer statements to read. Plus, you won't run the risk of forgetting to make a payment and being charged a fee if you only have two to keep track of!

Let's look at an example of the Net Worth Statement in action. Figure 3-2 shows the Net Worth Statement for a pair of clients, Caitlin and Peter. They've always had a hard time keeping track of things, so it took them a few hours to gather their information, but the results were worthwhile, because right off the bat I "found" them another $3,077 a year.

Looking at their Net Worth Statement, I discovered a few areas where their money could work harder for them right away. Each year they pay over $21,000 to service their debt. For instance, they have a $75,000 line of credit on

FIGURE 3-2.
SAMPLE NET WORTH STATEMENT.

Assets:	Rate:	Liabilities:	Rate:	Cost:
Home: $450,000	5%	Mortgage: $250,000	6.5%	$ 16,250
401(k): $125,000	8%	Home Equity: $25,000	5.75%	$ 1,437
401(k): $145,000	9%	Car Loan: $30,000	6.5%	$ 1,950
Roth IRA: $8,000	3%	Student Loan: $11,500	6.0%	$ 690
Roth IRA: $7,400	3%	Credit Cards: $9,300	15.0%	$ 1,395
Checking: $53,500	1%			
Savings: $10,000	3%			
Mutual Funds: $48,200	5%			
Cars: $32,300	0%			
Jewelry: $31,000	0%	(no plans to sell)		
Furniture: $27,500	0%			
Annual Cost of Debt:				$ 21,722
TOTAL ASSETS: $937,900		**TOTAL LIABILITIES:**		**$325,800**
Caitlin and Peter's Net Worth:				**$612,100**

their home equity loan on which they're paying 5.75 percent and receiving a tax deduction. (In their tax bracket, the cost of borrowing this money is 3.73 percent.) They're only using $25,000. So the first thing I recommended was to pay off the car loan and credit cards with their home equity line. That means instead of paying $3,345 every year to service this debt of $39,300 ($30,000 for the car loan at 6.5 percent, non-tax-deductible, and $9,300 at 15 percent non-tax-deductible), they will now pay $2,259 a year

($39,300 at 5.75 percent) through the home equity line. Then, after they use their tax deduction, their real cost is $1,465. So if you were borrowing $39,300 every year, how much would you rather pay to borrow? Would you choose $3,345 or $1,465? Caitlin and Peter are enjoying a savings of $1,880 this year, and it's an easy process.

I also noticed that they kept a high balance in their checking account, which was earning only one percent interest from their bank. Just by moving $40,000 to savings, they'd earn another $1,200 per year. And if they use a tax-free savings account, as I recently recommended, their return will be even better.

Can you see how creating the Net Worth Statement can really pay off for you? Caitlin and Peter "found" $3,080 just by putting their Net Worth Statement together!

CUSTOMIZE THE NET WORTH STATEMENT FOR *YOU!*

When you start a new diet and exercise regimen, you do little things to keep yourself motivated—to remind yourself of the reason you're passing up those potato chips and getting up a half-hour earlier in the morning to go running. You tape a picture of your favorite soccer star to your mirror; you keep a flyer for that marathon on your fridge. With your financial goals, as with your health goals, it helps to keep your eyes on the prize.

Over the past six years, two things have always made the Net Worth Statement fun for my clients. First, they can see the increase in their net worth from year to year, and that gives them a terrific sense of accomplishment and peace of mind. Second, I ask that they *make* it fun. I suggest that underneath their total net worth number they write categories, such as: Special Days for Me, Special Family Events, Work Milestones, Books I Read, Friends I Saw, Movies, Trips, and so forth. The reasons for adding these personal statements are twofold:

1. *Adding personal memories makes the experience more pleasant.* It gets you pumped up about the experiences you're having and the people you're having them with.

2. *The experiences you choose to write indicate your true priorities—and point the way to your true goals.* They're an indicator of what your money is really there to serve. Because, as I'm about to explain, the main goal behind all your financial efforts is to support what really matters.

YOUR GOALS

Now we've come to the fun part: deciding where you want to be in the future—or, put another way, identifying point B. Just as you'd determine how many pounds you needed to lose to get in shape, or how much speed and stamina you needed to gain for a particular athletic event, you'll now identify your financial goals.

In this section, I'll walk you through the process of establishing reasonable and achievable financial aims, taking into account your personal values, interests, and concerns. I'll help you identify your short-term goals for the next three to six months, which might be setting up an emergency reserve; medium-term goals for the next six months to five years, such as taking an extended leave of absence from your job; and long-term goals, such as buying a home or saving for retirement. By the time you're finished with this section, you'll have confidence that the goals you've set are the ones that matter most to you and are 100 percent doable within your current circumstances.

You'll probably enjoy this part of the process. Did you know that goal setting gives you a natural high? Research has shown that when you set and pursue goals, your brain releases the chemical dopamine. As you identify goals and move toward them, you'll actually feel better. You'll experience a sense of well-being and success. Having a goal isn't about achieving a *thing*; it's about feeling empowered and taking control of where you are going. Having goals helps you get through even the most difficult times.

But, to get the full benefit of setting and pursuing goals, we have to make sure that they're really the right goals for you. Your goals must be motivated by the right reasons. Goals that are motivated by comparison to what others have, by the expectations of others, or by fears and worries are destined to fail, because the wrong motivations are driving them. Let's examine each of these three "false motivators" in turn.

False Goal 1: Comparison to Others

It's all too easy in today's world to choose goals for ourselves that don't truly reflect our values and priorities. The media, society, family, friends, and colleagues can influence us into believing that our goals should be geared toward creating a lifestyle that *looks* successful. Our need to be admired by others can easily derail us from our true goals.

Psychologists call this phenomenon "reference anxiety." When you use other people's level of success as a gauge for your own, or any time you see someone who's outwardly more successful than you are, you experience anxiety. You will *always* see people who are more successful than you are—just as you'll always see people who have better muscles, lower body fat, and more stamina. So if you base your success on how you compare to others, you're setting yourself up for a lifetime of stress.

The silly thing about reference anxiety is that it has no internal reference of its own. It's all about what you see around you. Let's say you own a two-bedroom home. As long as everyone else around you owns a two-bedroom home, your reference anxiety is low and you're fine. But plop that same home down in a neighborhood with three- and four-bedroom homes, and suddenly that house that seemed perfectly adequate to you before becomes a source of embarrassment. Your sense of well-being is threatened. You may begin to run up your credit cards trying to keep up with the Joneses, which will only increase your anxiety.

If you go into a gym with a clear idea of what *you* want to become, both in the short and long term, you won't be distracted by other people's conditions. Your financial goals are no different. They must be goals that you choose for yourself, rather than goals that look good on someone else.

False Goal 2: Expectations of Others

I had a friend whose father pushed him to get into football. He went to practice all through high school only because he wanted to please his dad. But his real love was for soccer. In spite of his best efforts, he was only a so-so football player. Who knows how far his passion might have driven him if he'd followed his desire and played soccer instead?

Maybe your parents had high hopes for you financially. Did they dream of the day you'd be a high-powered lawyer, an entrepreneur, or a neurosurgeon? Did they brag that you'd make your first million before the age of thirty?

If this sounds like you, it's time to free yourself from the burden of living up to the expectations of others. Even though you might be able to achieve the standards others have set for you, you'll find when you get there that the victory rings hollow.

Your goals must be *your* goals, not the ones other people have set for you.

False Goal 3: Freedom from Worry

What made you pick up this book? Was it because you're frustrated over being up to your eyeballs in credit card debt? Are you overwhelmed with a feeling of responsibility, working to pay your mortgage and put something away for the future each month? Are you terrified that some unexpected expense will descend upon you and wipe out your emergency reserves? Or maybe you're tired of feeling that your financial life is out of control. Your financial statements are all over the place, you never have a clear idea of how your money's doing, and there's an atmosphere of chaos hanging over your financial future.

These are all legitimate concerns, but they're not what I want you to focus on, at least for now. Fear is not a positive driver. It can't yield the same level of results you can get from inspiration. You're much more likely to succeed if you're working *toward* something you *do* want, rather than working to avoid something you don't want.

Your goal cannot simply be "to alleviate my financial worries." But we do need to deal with your fears in order to clear the path toward your true goals. Conquering fears is not a goal in itself; it's one objective toward your goals.

TRUE GOALS: REFLECTIONS OF PERSONAL VALUES

I tell my clients this all the time: You have to be honest about what you want for yourself. Otherwise, your desire won't be intense enough to help you reach your goals. Achieving goals takes passion, and living up to other people's expectations can't possibly generate enough passion.

If you really want to master handling your money, you have to start from the inside out. Your goals must be consistent with who you are; they must serve your values.

Most people are confused about their values and goals, so they keep waffling back and forth, accomplishing very little. When you go after what you truly want, you'll have all the energy of true passion behind you.

I want you to do the Net Worth Workout because you

want to, not because you feel you have to. And the only way you'll want to do the workout badly enough to stick with it is to use it as a tool for achieving what you want most in life.

Even if you only accomplish one financial goal this year, follow the Net Worth Workout. It will benefit you and your finances in so many different ways—and it will be a boon to *any* goal you set for yourself. But the way to get the most out of your efforts, and the way to give yourself the best chance of sticking with it for the long haul, is to approach it from the deepest of motivations: getting in touch with your personal values.

Your values, which may include such attributes as compassion, generosity, and loyalty, determine your beliefs. They govern how you feel about yourself and the world— including the way you feel about money. Personal values such as frugality, charity, honesty, persistence, and excellence are the deepest possible motivations behind your goals. When your goals are in harmony with these principles, you're tapping into the deepest drives that you possess. Using Figure 3-3, start to clarify your values by writing them down and getting better perspective on them.

Make Goals Meaningful

In and of itself, having goals is no great feat. If you set the goal of staying home and watching television every day for a month, you could make it happen. It might feel nice, at least for the first few days, but at the end of the month, you'd probably be feeling unfulfilled.

FIGURE 3-3.
CLARIFY YOUR VALUES.

What are the three or four most important values in your life today?

1. _____
2. _____
3. _____
4. _____

What qualities and values are you best known for among your friends and colleagues?

1. _____
2. _____
3. _____
4 _____

Describe your idea of the person you would most want to be if you had no limitations.

_____

_____

_____

_____

What changes would you make today to help you live in greater harmony with your values?

1. _____
2. _____
3. _____

Goals aren't worth much unless they're meaningful. They're also much harder to achieve if you don't feel the meaning in them. Write the answers to the following questions and your true goals will be staring you in the face.

What means the most to you in life?

_____

_____

In the past six months, what were your "high points?"

_____

_____

What makes you identify these moments as high points?

_____

_____

Your "definitive goals"—the things you desire from the very core of your being, the wants and intentions that make you who you are—have been with you all your life, even though you may not be aware of them.*

We grown-ups are too easily distracted from what's really important. I can't imagine my six-year-old niece, Caroline, describing her definitive goal as owning a ski chalet, but she might say spending more time with her best friend Megan or being able to ski as much as possible. For Caroline, as for most of us, it's about events and people rather than about things. We're more likely to be happy when people take precedence over things.

What is your overarching definitive goal? Perhaps you

*The definitive source on definitive goals is Michael Ray's *The Highest Goal*, San Francisco, Berrett-Koehler, 2004.

have a few. For me, it's being a teacher. Helping people understand their money and feel less intimidated by it, and ultimately giving them more time with the people they love, is what fires me up.

Your financial goals, and all other goals, should point to your highest purpose in life. Take the time to explore your definitive goal. Is it to spend more time with your family? To be your own boss and create something special? To give back to society? Write it down and explain why it's central to the person you are.

My definitive goal is:

_____

_____

Make Sure It's a *Goal,* Not Just a Dream

In the previous section, I directed you to identify your definitive goal. But chances are, what you've answered is not yet a true goal. It's a dream. It's healthy to have dreams; without them there is no vision for the future and long-range incentives. But many of us confuse a dream with a goal. Making a lot of money, spending more time with your family, and being happy aren't goals; they're dreams. It doesn't become a goal until you identify what's necessary to bring it about. For instance, a high school baseball player may dream of playing professional ball, but that's not his goal. One of his goals may be to beat his batting average this season.

A goal is clear, written, and specific. It should stretch you and be positive. You can measure it and know precisely whether it has been achieved. You should also be aware of your limitations. Someone who wants to get fit may say their limitation is that they don't have much aerobic endurance. Likewise, if you're trying to save money, your limitation may be that you charge too much on your credit cards, or have a lot of credit card debt to pay off first. You cannot achieve a goal through sheer willpower; you can only achieve it through systematic action.

Most goals require several steps and contain a number of components. And one major component in nearly every worthwhile goal is money.

THE FINANCIAL ASPECT OF YOUR GOALS

The proper role of money in your life, then, is as a tool for achieving your true goals. Money is a facilitator for the things that matter most to you. Money is not a goal in and of itself; it is one part of the journey toward a goal. The way I explain it to my clients is that money is just like that pair of running shoes you need to run a race—it's a piece of equipment.

Let's say, for instance, that you identify friendship as one of your core values. Your dream is to spend more time with the friends who matter to you most. You and your friend Ann have talked for years about taking a walking tour of Tuscany—that's still a dream. The day you say you're going to take that trip in May 2008, it becomes a goal. When you start choosing exactly which cities you'll visit, when you're going to book the tickets and make the decision about who's going to water the philodendrons while you're gone, you're making a plan. When you work out exactly how much money you'll need for the trip and how you plan to save up that money over the next year, you're working on the financial aspect of your goal.

Consider the financial aspect of some of the goals listed here:

Definitive Goal:	Financial Aspect:
Caring for children	College tuition
Caring for elderly parent	In-home nurse visits
Social cause/religious mission	Charitable foundation
Entreprencurial vision	Start-up capital

The best way to keep money in proper perspective is to remain focused on the people and experiences that make your life worthwhile. Your financial life exists to serve the things that matter most to you.

Short-Term, Medium-Term, and Long-Term Financial Goals

Your goals will be more manageable if you divide them into three categories: short, medium, and long.

Your short-term goals are things that you can reasonably accomplish, under normal circumstances, in the next three to six months. They may include getting your money organized through the Net Worth Workout, paying off your credit card debt, buying that plasma TV, or building up three to six months' worth of living expenses.

Your medium-term goals take a bit longer: six months to five years. Perhaps you're saving for a wedding, buying a new car, working toward saving 10 percent of your income, starting a business, or taking a year off.

Your long-term goals are the ones I call the Big Three: saving for your child's education, funding a retirement, and buying a home. Though it may take you a few years to save to buy a home, it's a long-term goal because it takes many more years to pay it off! Be sure that you don't neglect the Big Three when choosing your goals. Oppenheimer provides some useful goal analysis tools on its website. See Appendix B for samples you can put to use right now.

The next step is to make sure you have prioritized your goals. I always advise my clients to start with the Big Three, then do a little in each area, rather than concentrating all their efforts in one. I recommend this approach because the choices you make regarding one goal can easily affect your ability to achieve another. Think about what we learned in Chapter Two about opportunity cost. If you're saving to buy a new boat (or any "big-ticket" dream item), it's going to pull resources from saving for retirement. Plenty of people have comfortable retirements without ever having a boat, and they usually get there quicker! Is boat ownership worth delaying retirement for a few more years?

It's similar to entering a race. You arrive at the site, see old pals, and meet great people, and before you know it, the social aspect distracts you. Or maybe you're tempted to stay up late the night before the race, having a few drinks with your friends. But if you do, your performance will suffer, and you'll feel disappointed about your performance.

In short, you need to keep your eye on the prize—the prize that's most important to you.

Use Figure 3-4 to prioritize your short-, medium-, and long-term goals and the financial implications of each.

YOUR PLANS

Once you've identified point A and point B, your next step is to chart the course between them. This section helps you develop a strategy for achieving your goals.

In my athletic endeavors, I have met many types of people: individuals who accomplish nearly every goal they set for themselves, as well as those who can't seem to get around to setting any goals. The difference between those who procrastinate and those who don't comes down to a single principle: Those who achieve their goals follow a routine. The others tell themselves things like "I'm not in the mood," or they say they'll enter that race or join that team when they get into better shape, yet they make no provisions for getting in better shape.

If you hear yourself making comments such as these, chances are you're a procrastinator. When you put off things like paying your bills, studying your investments, or getting that run in, stress hormones are released in your body. Those stress hormones can wear out your body faster and even weaken your immune system. It's one of the reasons why handling our money can be so stressful and emotional.

FIGURE 3-4. CLARIFY YOUR GOALS.

Short-Term Goals

List three things you'd like to achieve in the next three to six months, and the financial implications of those goals. For instance, if your goal is to enroll your seven-year-old prodigy in violin lessons, write the dollar amount per month you have to commit to meet this goal.

Goal   Financial Aspect of Goal

1. _____   _____
2. _____   _____
3. _____   _____

Medium-Term Goals

List three things you'd like to achieve in the next six months to five years, and the financial implications of those goals. Let's say you want to spend next summer in Ireland exploring your family's genealogy. Write the total cost of airfare, hotel, meals out, transportation, and time lost from work.

Goal   Financial Aspect of Goal

1. _____   _____
2. _____   _____
3. _____   _____

Long-Term Goals

List three things you'd like to achieve in the next five to twenty years, and the financial implications of those goals. That house you want to buy in two years—how much must you set aside for your down payment?

Goal   Financial Aspect of Goal

1. _____   _____
2. _____   _____
3. _____   _____

But when it comes to organizing your money, you don't need to "feel like doing it"—most of us don't! One of the greatest lies we tell ourselves is that we'll surely feel more motivated about handling our money tomorrow. Or next week. Or next month. It's exactly what we told ourselves when we were on all those diet plans that failed.

You don't have to be "in the mood" to do the work. In fact, it's the opposite. You don't wait to act until the mood hits; you act and then the mood comes to you. Remember flow theory, from Chapter Two? You achieve the state of flow by getting into your task.

To keep yourself on task, then, you need to develop a plan of action that you will be able to follow. This three-step exercise will help you to chart a plan of action for achieving your goals.

Goal Planner

1. Make a list of the goals you identified previously: that is, your short-, medium-, and long-term goals.

2. Break each goal into specific tasks.

3. For each goal, identify where the necessary resources (e.g., time, money, and equipment) will come from.

Let's use an example to show how this goal planner looks in action. Steven and Claire were very motivated to articulate their goals. Financial concerns had been hanging over their heads for several years, and they were anxious to "get going"—especially since they had three teenage children. Their short-term goals, listed by priority, were to:

1. Complete their first Net Worth Statement.

2. Consolidate their six credit cards down to two.

3. Put six months of living expenses into savings.

Their medium-term goals were to:

1. Put aside 7 percent of their gross income for college.

2. Set up a 529 plan (a college investment account) for each of their three kids.

3. Set aside funds to renovate and build a media room.

Their long-term goals were to:

1. Invest 10 percent of their gross income toward retirement.

2. Refinance their mortgage to pay it off over 20 instead of 30 years.

3. Set aside $2,500 a year to buy long-term care insurance.

Once they identified their goals, the next step was to break down each goal into tasks. To "set aside funds to renovate and build a media room," for example, the tasks were to:

- Get three quotes from contractors and an estimate of how much time it will take.

- Get pricing for the television, stereo, and cabinetry.

- Choose the contractor and equipment that best suits their needs.

Their next step was to identify where the necessary resources would come from. They decided to budget for their new media room by:

- Setting aside $200 a month next year to pay for some of it.

- Setting aside their annual bonuses and their tax refund of $10,000 to pay for the rest.

I'm happy to report that Steven and Claire are on schedule to start their remodeling project this spring. They've already picked out the model of wide-screen TV that will grace their new room when it's complete, and they're thrilled. The kids are ecstatic, too. Before Steven and Claire did this exercise, they believed their media room would have to wait until the kids were grown and out of college. They were so overwhelmed by their larger financial goals that they couldn't conceive of a shorter-term, "just for fun" goal. Once they outlined all their goals, large and small, and got down to the nuts and bolts of how to make them happen, they realized that both goals were within their reach.

THE IMMEDIATE PAYOFF: YOUR SECRET WEAPON IN THE BATTLE TO KEEP YOUR GOALS ON TRACK

Throughout this chapter, you've probably enjoyed the natural high that comes from targeting your dreams and desires and turning them into goals. But somewhere about now, you may get hit with a sobering thought: "What if I can't stick with these plans? Last time I started a diet, I was bingeing on pizza within a week. What makes me think I can be any more disciplined with money?"

I understand why you feel this way—trust me; it's normal. We've all started out to achieve something, only to have our motivation fizzle. Our motivation fails us for a specific reason. Let me explain:

If you were offered the choice of $10 today or $11 tomorrow, which would you choose? Most people would choose the lower amount today. But if you were given the choice between $10 in a year and $11 in a year and one day, which would you choose? Most people would choose the higher, delayed amount.

The reason you and I (and everyone else) agonize over the choice between pizza today or lean thighs a month from now is that two different areas of your brain are fighting each other. These two areas—let's call them emotion and logic—compete for your decision between short-term wants and long-term goals. Your emotional brain wants to max out the credit card, vegetate on the couch, and order dessert. Your logical brain knows you should save for retirement, go for a run, and skip dessert.

Think you can just deny the part of your brain that's clamoring for dessert? Think you can beat it into submission with sheer willpower? Let me ask you: How well has this thinking worked for you in the past?

Again, you're not weak-willed; you're normal. Your desire for short-term gratification is simply part of being human. If your need for immediate joy is overpowering, my solution is to give in to it. Make short-term gratification part of your plan from the beginning. Just make sure you focus on the kind of gratification that *serves* your goals instead of derailing them.

I hate getting on the treadmill each morning. I'd much rather lounge in bed for that extra fifteen minutes. And trust me, it doesn't help one bit to try to motivate myself with visions of how fit I'll be next June if I get on the treadmill this morning in February. The only thing that gets me on the treadmill today is thinking about what it will do for me *today*. After fifteen minutes on the treadmill, I'll be in a better mood, have a clearer mind, and will bounce into my day with far more energy than if I skipped the morning workout. (I'll also have a sense of accomplishment, rather than feelings of guilt for missing a workout.) If I think of it this way, I'll opt to give myself the present of a happier morning. And the great shape I'll be in next June is an added bonus.

I want you to do the exact same thing with your financial goals: Focus on the immediate gratification. To see your goals through to success, you must shift your focus away from distant outcomes (e.g., saving enough for retirement) and instead concentrate on experiences you can have today that will make you feel good (e.g., saving money on your credit cards). Get in the habit of thinking this way. Then, whenever it's time to handle your money, you'll be eager to sit down and do it. You'll look forward to the natural high your financial sessions give you. They'll be a treat instead of a burden.

Additionally, give yourself little rewards all along the

way to your goals. If you're a gardener, treat yourself to fifteen minutes outside with your tomato plants at the end of each financial session. If you love movies, take yourself to the theater whenever you reach a financial benchmark. Associate all the financial planning you do with imminent pleasures. When you see the workout as a series of little joys on the way to bigger joys, you'll remain motivated enough to achieve even the longest-term goals.

■ ■ ■

In this chapter, you've drawn up your blueprint for financial success. You've assessed your current financial condition. You've identified the goals that are most important to you, and you've mapped out the steps that will take you there. You're now ready to put your plans into action by using the four quadrants approach (as covered in Chapter One) as your "core training." In the next chapter, you'll begin putting your finances through the Net Worth Workout, with the goal of making your money work as hard as it possibly can to make your dreams come true. Our first area of focus will be your income: We'll look at ways to get the most out of all aspects of your financial compensation.

EARNING: WHICH GEAR ARE YOU IN?

AS CHAPTER ONE ESTABLISHED, your net worth is generated by your activity in four financial quadrants: earning, spending, saving, and investing. Each of these quadrants relates to an aspect of physical fitness. Earning relates to metabolism, spending to nutrition, saving to strength training, and investing to cardiovascular training.

Earning, the first quadrant, can be likened to your metabolism because, just as a healthy metabolism increases the flow of energy throughout your body, a healthy income increases the flow of money throughout your life. In this chapter, we'll rev up your financial metabolism. I'll help you explore ways to increase your current income, maximize your benefits package, and even create income *from* income.

In this chapter, you'll analyze every aspect of your earning power. You'll learn that benefits (e.g., health care, day care, disability, and so forth) hold the key to your true earning capacity. So do your bonuses, 401(k) matches, stock options, dividends, interest, rental income, alimony, Social Security payments, and more. Every aspect of your earning gives power to your finances.

Throughout our work, bear in mind that none of the financial quadrants work in isolation. They're a team. They'll work hardest for you when you combine your efforts in each area. When you're trying to get in shape, you'll meet with some small success even if you *just* eat a sensible diet or *just* jog a mile every day. But you'll get the greatest payoff from combining a smart eating plan with regular exercise, muscle building, and cardiovascular work.

The high-quality diet revs your metabolism, provides materials for muscle building, and creates a reliable energy source for cardiovascular workouts. A speedy metabolism routes the nutrition from your healthy diet to your hard-working heart, lungs, and muscles. Those muscles you build during weight lifting help to burn fat even when you're at rest. And your cardiovascular workout maximizes muscle building and boosts your metabolism. Just as these four body systems work in concert, so the four financial quadrants work to support each other.

THE MAGIC OF METABOLISM: CREATING INCOME FROM INCOME

Have you ever noticed those people in the gym, or in your yoga, spinning, or kick-boxing class, who don't seem to be working out any harder or longer than you, but they're in better shape? Perhaps you have a friend like that. She eats the same way you do. Yet she never gains a pound. What gives?

The difference is that her workouts target and raise her metabolism.

Metabolism is the way—and the rate at which—your body burns energy to function. Your metabolism regulates the way your heart pumps blood around your body, the way you digest food, and the way your cells grow. A higher metabolism can help you stay healthier, just as income that is working more efficiently for you can generate more income. Our metabolic rates make up the majority of energy our bodies use, and some bodies are better at burning energy than others! But that is because those bodies (aside from genetics) have been trained better.

If you can increase your metabolic rate and keep eating the same amount of calories, you will lose weight. One way to increase metabolism is through strength training. This benefit is possible at any age. Scientists at Tufts University found that people in their nineties who did strength-training for eight weeks were able to alter their metabolism and increase their strength by 300 percent!

You can do the same with your income, no matter what

your age or income is. I'm going to show how you can increase your "income metabolism"—that is, how to make your income earn even more for you. Then you can sit back and enjoy the fruits of your labor, provided you continue to do your weekly "financial sessions."

YOU EARN THREE TYPES OF INCOME

Do you want to continue working forty, fifty, or sixty hours a week for the rest of your life? Or would you like to be able to take time off when you wish without worrying how your bills will be paid?

If you're like many people, your concept of income-earning is tied to the number of hours you work. If you don't log in the hours, you don't bring home the bacon. I'm going to show you that, to the contrary, the most powerful way to earn income is *not* by punching a time clock. Remember that the real benefit of a speedy metabolism is that it works for you even while you're at rest. Wouldn't it be nice if your income could do that—bring in money, even when you're not working?

It can.

The truth is you don't earn only one type of income. You earn three:

   ■ *Active income* is income for which you have performed some service—your wages, tips, salary, commissions, and income from businesses in which you have material participation. Let's say that when you're actively earning an income, it's analogous to the time you spend working out to increase your metabolism. The time you spend pursuing active income is the time you spend sweating! Use the spaces below to list your active income:

Wages: _____

Tips: _____

Salary: _____

Commissions: _____

Other: _____

Total Active Income: _____

- *Passive income* comes from rental property, limited partnerships, or other enterprises in which you are not actively involved. You've heard of the studies that show that after you've exercised, you continue to reap the benefits for several hours afterward, and if you exercise regularly, you'll enjoy better health, higher energy, and a host of other rewards. It's likewise with passive income. As long as you put some of that active income to work for you, you'll benefit from an increased flow of money, even when you're not at work! List your passive income:

  Source   Amount

  _____   _____

  _____   _____

  _____   _____

  Total Passive Income: _____

- *Portfolio income* comes from investments, including dividends, interest, royalties, and capital gains. Just as a higher metabolism helps you gain muscle mass, cardiovascular strength, and optimal absorption of nutrients, these benefits in turn enhance your metabolism. When you invest a portion of your earned income, the result is higher income! List your portfolio income:

Source   Amount

_____   _____

_____   _____

_____   _____

_____   _____

Total Portfolio Income: _____

In fact, your goal should be to gradually replace the first type of income with returns from the other two. If you look at millionaires and multimillionaires in this country, most of their earnings come from passive and portfolio income, some of which can be tax-free. On the other hand, most people's income comes from active income—all of which, typically, is taxable. One of the ways I would like to help you is to create more passive and portfolio income so your bills can be paid, you can work less, and you can spend more time with your family and friends!

This idea is the heart of the Net Worth Workout.

ACTIVE EARNING POWER: YOUR MOST IMPORTANT ASSET

Passive and portfolio earnings may be the "magical" sources of income, but unless you're a trust fund baby or you hit the lottery, they draw all their strength from active earnings: the money you earn from sweating nine to five. In the absence of "found" money, your active income is the fuel that makes the other two powerhouses go.

What if I were to ask you to name your greatest asset? If you're like many of my clients, your answer might be your home, 401(k) plan, investment accounts, perhaps even your car or a piece of artwork. But the truth is, it's your ability to earn a living. Sure, you may live in a home that's worth $250,000 or have over $300,000 in investment assets. But if you're thirty-eight years old, earn the typical income of $43,000, and plan to work until you're sixty-seven, then your "asset" is $1,247,000—not assuming any raises! What else do you have that is worth so much?

That's why I strongly recommend that you have disability insurance. You have health insurance to take care of your body if it becomes sick; doesn't it make as much sense to take care of your income-earning power, if it should become "sick"? Over 65 percent of mortgages default because of a disability. We insure our homes, cars, artwork, and jewelry, but most of us neglect our most important asset: our ability to earn a living! And if you're paid in company stock, you should also look into hedging strategies to protect that stock.

We want to protect our active earning power and strengthen it as much as we can. I want you to earn as much as possible from your job, but keep in mind that maximizing your income means more than the number of zeros on your W2. I know people with four zeros who have much more financial security than those with five! How is this possible?

Perhaps you're one of those people who thinks that if you earn a bigger paycheck, your money issues will go away. Ask yourself how you lived when you were twenty-five. Are you earning more than you were then? Most of us are. Have your financial problems been alleviated because you're earning more now? Then what makes you think anything will change as you earn more in the next five years?

It's not the number of digits in your paycheck that makes you financially strong. It's what you're doing with the money you have.

A similar principle is at work in fitness. It is possible to lose twenty pounds and still be flabby and weak if the weight you lost is all muscle. On the other hand, it is possible to lose only ten pounds and look and feel great if twenty pounds of fat are lost and ten pounds of muscle are gained!

Even though I want you to bring home the biggest paycheck you can, your ability to affect the amount of your paycheck isn't as great as your ability to change the way you use your benefits. For the majority of this chapter, we'll focus on your total benefits and compensation package, because that's where you have the most potential to raise your financial fitness.

Many employers are concerned with helping you balance your work and life, especially if they aren't able to get you that merit raise you've been waiting for. Thanks to a growing awareness of the frictional costs inherent in employee turnover, the trend is toward subsidies for expenses once considered "strictly personal"—for instance, adoption, on-site day care, and museum admissions, to name a few. It's time to capitalize on whatever offerings you can.

Do you know if your company offers flextime, tuition reimbursement, elder care, long-term care—even pet insurance? Is there an on-site gym? Maybe you can buy birthday cakes from the company cafeteria and save the expense of a bakery.

Once you've seen your entire earnings-and-benefits package, you can weigh it against your goals and determine the changes you need to make. Then, with your financial metabolic shift under way, you'll start to feel your "energy level" climb—and, chances are, you'll sleep better at night.

LET'S CHECK YOUR FINANCIAL METABOLISM

How much will you make this year? Don't tell me you don't know.

It's funny how often I ask clients what their total household income is and get a blank look as a response. Sure, many people can tell me what *they* earn in a year, but when it comes to their spouses, the answer often becomes a bit fuzzy. Or perhaps you work on commission in an uncertain, cyclical industry—or you're self-employed.

When new clients tell me they don't know their own annual income, I usually reply with something friendly, like, "Well, is it closer to $10,000, or $1 million?" Some people won't even answer that!

What are they hiding? Most of the time, they're either embarrassed by their situation or concerned that I'll know too much about their business. It probably feels the same as when your doctor asks you to disrobe for your annual physical. You feel funny about it, but your doctor just wants to do the job right.

But whether you tell me or not, don't be so embarrassed that *you* don't know what you really earn! Please be frank with yourself in this exercise.

In Chapter Three, you completed your Net Worth Statement. Now, let's do some "light lifting," to stimulate and assess your metabolism. Your first exercise goes like this: Stand up. Stretch! Now walk over to your desk and pick up a three-ring binder. You'll need this binder for a number of upcoming exercises, so this is a good time for you to begin practicing the binder-lift.

Please make sure your binder has tabs to separate your sections. In the first section, put the Net Worth Statement you created in Chapter Three. Keep it and all subsequent quarterly statements in this section, so you'll always know what you have to work with. This may seem tedious, but remember, it's how we're going to bring hundreds or thousands of dollars to your bottom line, so it's worth the effort!

In the second section, which you should label "Income," place a copy of last year's W2 and your most recent tax return. Then add your most recent pay stub and, if you are married, your spouse's most recent pay stub. If you are self-employed, commissioned, or receive bonuses, include those payment records, too. This exercise gives you a sense of your monthly gross and net income.

What's the difference between gross income and net income? Gross income is the total amount you make before taxes; net income is the total amount you make after taxes,

Social Security, health insurance, 401(k) contributions, etc., have been taken out.

Include all your dividends, W2, pension, real estate, and pay records from consulting or part-time jobs. To start, take out your most recent tax return. Then use the information on these documents to fill out the chart in Figure 4-1.

Record your gross income first, then your net income beside it.

Now that you have your annual figures, you're going to start generating monthly figures. What do you receive from your paycheck, Social Security, or pension every two weeks? What actually goes into your checking account, if you do direct deposit?

The easiest way to keep track of your monthly income is to store your pay stubs in your binder. Make it a warm-up to your weekly "financial session" to record the amount

FIGURE 4-1.
TOTAL ANNUAL INCOME.

	Me		My Spouse	
	Gross	Net	Gross	Net
W2 Income	_____	_____	_____	_____
Dividends	_____	_____	_____	_____
Alimony	_____	_____	_____	_____
Social Security	_____	_____	_____	_____
Pension	_____	_____	_____	_____
TOTAL	$_____	$_____	$_____	$_____

of income you and your spouse had that week. Then you simply add up the amounts at the end of each month. These monthly numbers are very important, because they will help us determine your lifestyle—which we'll discuss in Chapter Five, on spending.

Now let's see what we can do to pump up that financial metabolism and raise your income.

MAXIMIZE YOUR ACTIVE INCOME—TODAY

First, let's make sure you're earning as much as you should be. Are you getting adequate compensation for the work you do? Do you know what the average pay scale is for someone in your position?

It's very important to know what your value in the market is. You need to have an understanding of your industry and your expertise. And you need to appreciate what a resource your talents and good habits represent.

I'm sure that you've watched what you eat, at least at some point in your adult life. Most of us know how many calories or fat grams our favorite treat holds, if not how many grams of protein or fiber are in our "emergency ration" fast-food or frozen dinner. Maybe you view these choices in terms of how many extra minutes on the treadmill they'll cost you. Should you be any less discerning about your number-one asset, your ability to earn a living?

Amazingly, most people don't know their own worth! One journalist I know worked for the same publisher since graduate school. After almost ten years, he took a sabbatical to write his first book. To his amazement, prestigious offers started flowing in unsolicited. This was the first time he had any inkling of what his salary package should be.

Count on it: If you're unsure of your value, your company will underpay you! To get a feeling for your worth, ask yourself two questions: What is the salary range for this position? Which companies (or types of companies) should you compare your role to when determining salary for these positions?

If you're job searching, the same principle holds true. It's common to get wrapped up in the excitement of a job offer. But now is the time to negotiate all the extras, including a signing bonus, relocation expenses, and so forth. One way to increase your income is to trade your fixed pay for variable pay such as a bonus. And last, but certainly not least, if a company says it will do something financially in the future, *always* request it in writing! Some people may think it can jeopardize the relationship; it's more likely to solidify your future employer's respect for you!

I must stress again how important it is to view your income as something more than the dollars in your weekly paycheck. Since the typical American changes jobs every four years (that's eleven job changes over a forty-four-year career), it's vital that we discuss what I call "free agent syndrome."

Now, I'm not saying that you shouldn't take advantage of a great opportunity or find more challenging work to keep you growing. But many times I see people discount what they already have just to earn another $10,000 or $20,000, and often they don't realize what they're giving up in exchange. They may "trade teams" without knowing every ramification—especially if they're flattered by the bigger salary quoted. But at their new stadium, the manager may not play them as often, or may restrict their licensing deals. Will you get the same number of paid vacation days, the same perquisites?

A client of mine was considering moving to Atlanta for a management job. The hiring firm offered her the same amount of money—$100,000—saying that "the cost of living in Atlanta is significantly less than in New York City." However, at her current firm, my client receives 5 percent 401(k) match, as well as a 10 percent credit to her pension every year. The latter represents another $15,000 free and clear, something she would not receive from her new suitors.

Then, too, income is not just a matter of the dollar amount; it's also about how you *perceive* that dollar amount. Chapter 3 noted that people who live in two-bedroom homes are perfectly happy until their two-bedroom home is surrounded by three- and four-bedroom homes. Then they're unhappy.

The same thing happens with our income. Suppose you were asked to choose between living in two imaginary worlds *where the prices were the same.* In the first world you get $50,000 a year, while others get $25,000. In the second world, you get $100,000 a year, while others get $250,000.

Which would you prefer? The majority of a group of Harvard students preferred the *first!* They were happy to be poorer as long as they earned more relative to other people![1]

Now what if someone worked more and had less free time? In other words, does the same apply when it comes to time? The Harvard researchers gave the students the following two choices:

1. You have two weeks of vacation and others have one week.

2. You have four weeks of vacation and others have eight weeks.

Only 20 percent chose the first one. So people aren't envious of leisure time, but they are about income. This rivalry is self-defeating because it just makes you feel bad. Please, keep these ego issues front-of-mind whenever you evaluate a job offer.

MAXIMIZE YOUR FINANCIAL METABOLISM: TAKE ADVANTAGE OF BENEFITS

We just looked at your income in terms of its actual dollar amount. Now let's focus on your benefits—the great untapped gold mine of American wage-earners.

Did you know the typical employer spends an additional 20 percent to 40 percent of an employee's compensation providing them benefits? If you're thinking you'd rather have that amount in cash, you're not alone, but your employer reaps huge tax deductions from funding your benefits.

Most of us face the uncertainty of not knowing how secure our jobs are. Today, it's not unusual for companies to even reduce your income or not give you the typical inflation raise of 3 percent to 5 percent, and that's not very comforting. Worse yet, though it's there for the taking, most employees allow very large percentages of their income to go to waste—a significantly higher percent than the 3-to-5 percent bite of inflation—because they don't use most of their benefits.

At most companies, only 10 percent to 25 percent of employees take advantage of prepaid services like concierge or free legal services, etc. Can you guess why? Many human resources departments are thinly staffed and don't have the manpower to educate their employees. It's as if you vacationed at a fitness camp where the kitchens were stocked with healthy food, but there was no budget left over to hire nutrition coaches.

Whether or not your employer promotes its "healthiest options," let's start with the must-haves today. The first three benefits I tell my clients to sign up for are the health-care and child-care spending accounts, transportation spending, and company match. You might be tempted to dismiss these offerings, particularly the last two, because they're not cash. But think of it this way: These three expenses must be paid for one way or another. If you don't take advantage of the break you'll get through your employer, you'll have to surrender some of your hard-earned cash to pay these expenses out-of-pocket. If you think of your benefits this way, they start to seem like found money!

Let me give you an example. My client, Mark, was making a good income of $65,000 a year. But a young family and a long commute ate through his paycheck in no time. I tried to help him find ways to maximize his income so he would have more left over from each paycheck to invest. When we looked at his expenses, we learned that every year he and his wife paid at least $1,800 in health-care costs: the $500 deductible, prescriptions that weren't completely covered, contact lenses, and so forth. Then there was the cost of child care for their five-year-old daughter, which totaled more than $600 a month. The train pass to get Mark to work every day cost him $150 a month. When we reviewed his benefits, I told him he was wasting thousands of dollars every year. Of course he wanted to know why!

I suggested that he exert a little energy and boost his metabolism by setting up a flexible spending account (FSA), which would allow him to put away money, pretax, to pay for health-care expenses. In fact, Mark's employer would also allow him to use a child-care and transportation spending account. These accounts saved him a substantial sum, because he could get all the health-care, child-care, and transportation services he needed cheaper. Look at it this way: If you could buy an identical item, one costing $100 and another costing $65—and there wasn't any difference in quality—wouldn't you rather pay $65? It was the exact same thing for Mark when he began using these three spending accounts. Look at Mark's before-and-after figures. The numbers speak for themselves:

Paying After-Tax		Paying Using the Pretax Accounts	
Health-Care	$1,800	Health-Care Account	$1,800
Child-Care	$2,500	Child-Care Account	$2,500
Transportation	$1,800	Transportation	$1,800
After-Tax Cost	$6,100	Pretax Cost	$3,965

Now instead of paying $6,100 out of pocket, as Mark was doing when he paid for these items after tax, by paying pre-tax, he significantly reduced his costs. We saved him $2,135! We just helped Mark reduce his taxable income and pay less for the things he was buying on an after-tax basis.

That's step one. Step two: Turn income into income!

That "found" $2,135 in income can be redirected toward a college fund for his daughter's education or a retirement plan for him and his wife. Let's say Mark takes this $2,135 and invests it into a Roth IRA. (A Roth IRA is a retirement savings vehicle. The contributions aren't tax-deductible, but assuming all conditions are met, the money withdrawn is completely tax-free. Also, there is not a required minimum distribution after age $70^1/_2$.)

We'll assume that since Mark is thirty years old; he chooses a Roth IRA that invests in the S&P 500, where the average return has been 10 percent; and he continues to add another $2,135 to his account each year until he retires. When Mark reaches age sixty-seven, that Roth IRA will be worth $847,696. Tax-free!

That means Mark can generate a tax-free income of $33,907 per year for the rest of his life! (This figure assumes he pays out 4 percent and reinvests the rest to hedge against inflation.) This magic all happened by taking advantage of the spending accounts offered through his employer and a total investment of $78,995. That's the secret of income-generating income.

■   ■   ■

In this chapter, I've walked you through the first of the four financial quadrants. You've seen how income is analogous to metabolism, and you've learned how to measure it, how to rev it up, and how to make the most of its secondary benefits. You've come to see income not just in terms of its dollar amount, but also in terms of the whole picture of compensation and benefits. Now let's add the next phase of this workout. In Chapter 5, we'll move on to the second financial quadrant—spending.

NOTES

1. Richard Layard, *Happiness: Lessons from a New Science* (New Jersey: Penguin Press, 2005), p. 41.

SPENDING: WHAT KIND OF FUEL ARE YOU BURNING?

ONE OF THE MOST IMPORTANT ASPECTS of any physical health regimen is diet. A person who has a Krispy Kreme doughnut for breakfast, Taco Bell burritos for lunch, and takeout from the local Chinese restaurant for dinner, and then spends the rest of the evening sitting in front of the television, is going to find it very difficult to lose weight and stay in shape. On the other hand, a person who eats yogurt and granola for breakfast, a cup of soup and a turkey sandwich for lunch, and grilled fish and vegetables for dinner, and follows a structured exercise program, will find it easier to lose weight and feel a lot better as well.

Of course, everyone would like to be healthy, both physically and financially—and both dreams are achievable. The real question is, how do you get there? Why do some people enjoy good physical health for decades while others don't? Some of it has to do with chance (i.e., heredity and environment), but a lot of it has to do with making the right choices about food and exercise.

The same is true of money. Just as an unhealthy diet can lead to serious health problems such as heart disease, strokes, and cancer, a disorganized spending program can lead to serious financial problems, like having to work more years than you would like, having limited choices in where you send your children to college, and even being unable to afford good health care. And just as it is with your physical health, these long-term implications are driven by your daily habits.

To get your spending quadrant in shape, you need to look carefully at those daily habits: the way you spend money. Once you're aware of—and understand—your financial behavior, it becomes much easier to make the changes you need to make.

NOT ALL CALORIES—OR PURCHASES—ARE ALIKE

It's important for you to be aware of the financial decisions you make every day, and of the potential short- and long-term effects of those decisions. If you're trying to get in shape, you know you've got to train yourself to opt for the roasted turkey breast instead of the fried chicken, the green salad instead of the fries, and the whole-grain bagel instead of the doughnut. Your food choices—and your spending choices—determine how much energy and financial strength you'll have for the day, and what kind of physical and financial shape you'll be in tomorrow.

Think of your purchases as different types of calories. What you buy has a huge impact on both your present and future financial health. Remember how we discussed the opportunity cost of financial decisions? Let's say, for instance, that you need to buy a new car. You're looking at a Volkswagen Passat, with monthly payments of about $200, when a BMW convertible catches your eye. The Bimmer is a lot more money—nearly twice as much—but you can more or less afford it, so you go for it. Now you've got a really cool car that you can drive down the street with the top down, waving to your neighbors. But then your fifteen-year-old comes to you and says that all his friends have laptops with DVD drives and CD burners, and he'd like to have one, too. If you'd bought the Passat, you'd be able to pay for a new computer in five or six months. Now, though, unless you want to put it on your credit card—which is not a good idea—Junior's going to have to wait at least a year for the computer.

The other problem with "trading up" is that it leaves us wanting more. As long as most people in your neighborhood drive Passats or Fords, you'll feel pretty good in that BMW. But if the Bimmer becomes the "typical" neighborhood car, you'll feel much the same as when you're driving the Passat.

This is a pretty simple—and obvious—example of how

your spending habits affect your day-to-day lifestyle. What may be even more important, though, is how decisions you make today can affect the future. If, for instance, instead of spending that extra $200 every month on a car, you put that money into a college fund, your son might be able to go to a private university rather than a state-run school. Similarly, if at thirty-five, you start putting the money into a 401(k) and if it averages 10 percent a year, by the time you're sixty-five, you will have close to an additional $400,000 at your disposal.

Think of it this way: When it comes to saving, $1 spent today is equivalent to $6.07 saved for the future. The question you should ask yourself is, "Can I get $6.07 of use from this item?"

If you're serious about losing weight, you know you've got to burn more calories than you take in. There's no getting around that. And if you want to be financially secure, you've got to earn more money than you spend. There's just no other way to get there.

Unfortunately, many people—possibly as many as 50 percent of U.S. consumers—live by what economists call the Spending Rule of Thumb: We spend whatever we make, and we take on more debt when our incomes rise. In fact, this kind of thinking is embedded in our way of life. When people prosper, they buy nicer cars, bigger homes, fancier clothes, go out to eat more often, and so forth. It's one reason the average citizen owes over $8,000 on his credit cards. As a financial adviser based in New York City, I've seen it time and time again.

I once worked with a professional couple who together

earned more than $200,000 a year. You'd think that people with that kind of income would be financially secure, even in New York. But between the $50,000 a year they paid on the mortgage for their apartment, the $15,000 that went to tuition for each of their children, the $10,000 per month rental of their summer house, the $10,000 a year they spent in restaurants, and the $6,000 annual cost of trainers and beauty treatments, they were living on the edge.

One of the first mantras I learned as a financial adviser is, "It's not what you earn, it's what you keep." And how you spend your money, and what you spend it on, determine how much of it you get to keep.

THE GREAT SPENDING RIDDLE

Just as we have power over our food choices, we have power over our spending. But before we can exercise that power, we have to answer the Great Spending Riddle: What does your lifestyle cost per month? Once you've answered that question—and I'm about to show you exactly how you can do that—you'll be able to make changes that will let you maintain what's important to you while at the same time saving more money for the future.

One of the first things I ask when I meet a new client is how much she spends every month. Interestingly, more often than not, people can't say. Sometimes they'll take out a pen and paper and say, "Well, my mortgage is $1,500, real estate taxes are $350, electricity is $65, and the phone is $150. . . ." At that point I usually stop them. I know that adding up fixed expenses isn't going to answer the question. In fact, even when I don't stop them and they come up with a figure, it's almost invariably at least $500 to $1,000 less than the real amount. That's because when it comes to spending, fixed expenses are only part of the story.

The rest of the story is lifestyle.

What I mean by *lifestyle* is all the things we spend money on beyond the basics. If we go back to the food analogy, we're now talking about the butter on your bagel, the cream sauce on your chicken breast, and the extra dollop of blue cheese dressing on your salad. We go to the movies, we have our hair cut, and we go out for dinner. We also give gifts for holidays and birthdays, pay someone to mow the lawn, and buy clothes that need dry cleaning. All these expenses are very easy to underestimate. No wonder most clients say, "Gee, I don't know what the *real* number is."

The funny thing is that these lifestyle expenses can have a substantial effect on your finances, regardless of your annual income. As described in Tom Wolfe's *The Bonfire of the Vanities,* they can present problems even for the wealthy:

> Sherman and Judy arrived at the Bavardages' building on Fifth Avenue in a black Buick sedan, with a white-haired driver, hired for the evening from Mayfair Town Car, Inc. They lived only six blocks from the Bavardages, but walking was out of the question. So he had hired this car and the white-haired driver to drive them six blocks, wait three and a half or four hours, then drive them six blocks

home and depart. Including a 15 percent tip and the sales tax, the cost would be $197.20 or $246.50, depending on whether they were charged for four or five hours in all.

To make matters worse, the driver couldn't pull up to the sidewalk near the entrance because so many limousines were in the way. He had to double-park. Sherman and Judy had to thread their way between the limousines. Envy . . . envy . . . from the license plates Sherman could tell that these limousines were not hired. They were *owned* by those whose sleek hides were hauled here in them. A chauffeur, a good one willing to work long hours and late hours, cost $36,000 a year, minimum. Garage space, maintenance, and insurance would cost another $14,000 at least, a total of $50,000, none of it deductible. *I make a million dollars a year—and yet I can't afford that.*[1]

Our lust for luxuries beyond our financial grasp doesn't go away as our income rises. There will always be some things we can't afford. That double-chocolate cheesecake is just as tempting to those with ten pounds to lose as it is to those who've got to lose fifty.

There's actually one very easy way to figure out how much you spend. You just take your after-tax income and subtract what you've saved over the last year. But that can be hard to face. Plus, it doesn't tell you what you're spending your money on, and that's what you really need to know. Until you know that, you can't do anything about it.

What *does* help is to make a list of all your monthly expenses. When you do that, you can figure out exactly how much you're spending, and even more important, how you're spending it. Are you spending it on things that matter to you? This is an essential part of the Net Worth Workout, because spending is an integral part of your financial health. And if you don't have a clear understanding of every element of your finances, there's no way you can develop a clear and workable financial plan.

As you'll see, figuring out how much you're spending gives you a tremendous sense of control. In fact, according to *Money* magazine, control of your finances plays a bigger role in determining how happy you are than control of your job, health, friendships, or weight.

NUTRITIOUS SPENDING, CONDIMENT SPENDING, JUNK FOOD SPENDING

The Net Worth Workout divides monthly expenses into three types: fixed, variable, and discretionary. Think of your fixed expenses as your meat and potatoes, your variable expenses as blueberries in your cereal, and your discretionary income as treats or junk food.

Let's begin with the fixed expenses. Think of these essential expenses as your daily fiber, protein, and complex carbohydrate intake—the oatmeal you have for breakfast, the turkey sandwich at lunch, the salmon-and-salad dinner, and so forth. This part of your nutrient profile may not be particularly exciting, but you couldn't survive without it. Fixed expenses include:

- Housing

- Groceries

- Utilities

- Transportation

- Home/Health/Auto Insurance

- Medical/Dental

- Real Estate Taxes

- Child Care

These are the bare necessities for running a household, the things that, when we think about our needs, most people name first.

Then there are all the other things you spend money on but don't necessarily have to buy. The Net Worth Workout divides these items into two categories, the first of which is variable expenses. If variable expenses were food choices, they would be the things that make your meals tastier: the banana on your oatmeal, the lettuce and tomato on your sandwich, or your spring roll appetizer at dinner. They're the extras in life. In the world of expenses, they include things like:

- Wardrobe/Dry Cleaning

- Haircuts/Basic Grooming

- Cell Phone

■ Health, Golf, or Tennis Club Memberships

■ Personal Enrichment Classes (e.g., yoga, French, cooking, pottery, or the kids' swimming and dance lessons)

■ Consulting Fees (e.g., attorney, accountant)

■ Home Maintenance (e.g., repairs, alarm/pool service)

■ Gifts for—and Travel to—Social Obligations and Major Events

■ Banking/ATM Fees

Finally, there are your discretionary expenses—the real treats. If they were food choices, they'd be the Krispy Kreme doughnut for breakfast, the potato chips at lunch, or the brownie sundae at dinner. You absolutely *can* live without them, but there are plenty of times you deserve them—just not all in one day. Discretionary expenses include:

■ Salon Services (e.g., massages, manicures)

■ Entertainment (e.g., movies, videos/DVDs, sporting events, or arts performances)

■ Gambling (e.g., lottery tickets, card games, office football pools)

■ Restaurant/Bar/Club Meals (e.g., snacks, mixed drinks, and expensive wines)

- Recreational "Toys" (e.g., jet skis, pleasure boats, Harley-Davidsons)

- Collecting (e.g., antiques, guns, coins, wines)

- Vacations to Spas or Exotic Locales

YOU ARE WHAT YOU SPEND

You may be surprised to hear that, for many people, variable and discretionary expenses comprise as much as 40 percent of their monthly spending. Part of the problem is that, unlike our fixed expenses, we just don't realize how much we actually spend on these items. In fact, although most of us haven't noticed it, the ratio of variable and discretionary to fixed expenses has shifted substantially over the last several years. And that's at least partly because professional marketers have gotten better and better at what they do.

Marketing has become a science. Marketers study and pitch to us relentlessly. They field hundreds of thousands of surveys and watch miles of videotape to see what makes people buy. You've probably noticed that products aimed at children are always displayed at a child's eye level, where they can see them and pester you to buy them. You may have noticed, too, that essentials like milk are always at the far end of a grocery store or supermarket. That's not an accident. They're placed there so that you have to walk down a long store aisle and pass lots of other products before you reach the milk you're looking for. Marketers know that the more things you see, the more you're likely to buy.

In fact, more than two-thirds of grocery store shoppers buy on impulse. On the other hand, if you bring a list of things you need when you go shopping, you not only spend less time in the store, you also spend less money there. In his book *The Millionaire Mind,* Thomas J. Stanley notes that 84 percent of millionaires shop with a list.[2]

For many people, shopping is a leisure activity. Marketers know that, and take advantage of it. That's why many retail environments are engineered to be welcoming, comfortable, and intimate—like visiting a friend's home where you can just show up anytime. Banana Republic and Starbucks have plush furniture and cozy nooks. Pottery Barn plays cool CDs, while Victoria's Secret sets the mood with romantic scents. Cinnabon bakeries disperse the aroma of their delectable treats so you can't wait to buy one. And Niketown stores pipe in the sound of professional athletes playing basketball and lifting weights so you feel like you're on the court or at the gym—all you have to do is grab some Nike shoes and clothes and start working out. It's all designed to make you spend more money, and it works.

Another thing that influences how we spend our money is what I call the stress/spending paradox. We all feel stress at various times in our lives, and one of the ways many people deal with that stress today is by going on spending binges. In fact, this kind of impulse spending has reached epidemic proportions nationwide. Ask any marriage or debt counselor. We pamper ourselves, and our families, by purchasing a lot of things we don't really need and can't really afford. What happens, though, is that rather than reducing our stress levels, buying things we shouldn't buy makes us feel anxious about our financial situations. That, in turn, leads us to work harder than ever at our jobs, which only serves to create even more stress in our lives.

A good example of the stress/spending paradox comes from an episode of *Sex and the City*. Struggling writer Carrie breaks up with her boyfriend, then discovers that the apartment they've been renting is up for sale. Carrie wants to buy it, even though, as she confides to her friend Miranda, she doesn't know where the down payment will come from. Feeling lousy and wanting to cheer herself up, Carrie decides to go shopping, and takes Miranda into a designer shoe store with her. When Carrie continues to complain about not having any money, Miranda suggests that buying designer shoes may be what got her into this fix. "So I have a hundred pairs of shoes like this," Carrie says. "What difference would $4,000 really make?"

"No," answers Miranda, "you have a hundred pairs of $400 shoes. You've spent $40,000." Stunned, Carrie practically bolts from the store and its temptations. Determined, though, to find the money for the down payment, she resolves to shun taxis for buses, which she figures will save her $10 a day. But she soon realizes that at that rate it would take ten years for her to save all the money she'd need for the down payment. Feeling deprived, she quickly gives up, and it's obvious—at least to the viewer—that it's just a matter of time before she heads back to the store for another pair of shoes she doesn't need.

I must admit that even I'm not immune to the stress/spending paradox. Sometimes I spend more money than I want, usually when some planned activity falls through, or when I'm feeling tired or down. For instance, one day I was supposed to go cycling with friends, but the weather was miserable. Instead, one of my friends suggested a trip to Saks Fifth Avenue, where we spent two hours trying on cute outfits for the office and the beach—with matching shoes, of course. Before I knew it, I'd blown a few hundred dollars. Afterward, I was annoyed at myself for spending so much to feel good when it wasn't part of my financial plan. A two-hour bike ride would've made me just as happy, with the added bonus of burning calories instead of my credit card.

There's a positive side to this story, though: Now I'm more aware of the times that I'm vulnerable to binge spending. Now when it rains, I head to a spinning class and join my friends there.

THE LIFESTYLE LOG

Just as being aware of what you eat is the first step to controlling your diet, being aware of exactly what you spend is the first step to taking control of your expenses. You'd be surprised how little people actually know about their spending habits. I often hear clients say things like "I don't need much," or, "Aside from necessities, I really don't spend at all." Then, when I question them more closely, I discover that they spend much more money than they think, and that a very large proportion of their spending is for nonessentials. So, ace personal trainer that I am, I devised the Lifestyle Log.

The Lifestyle Log is a simple way to keep track of how you're actually spending your money. I've used this system with my clients for several years, and they've all found it to be easy to use, extremely practical, and very eye-opening. The log, as shown in Figure 5-1, is divided into three large sections for recording fixed, variable, and discretionary expenses—the financial equivalent of the foods needed to survive, the foods that make meals tastier, and the special treats that you sometimes allow yourself. To make the log easy to use, these three sections are further divided into smaller sections, representing various aspects of each of the types of expenses. But the log doesn't just provide a way to keep track of what you're spending on necessities and nonnecessities. It also enables you to keep track of *why* you're spending money on nonessential items, which is very important if you want to change your spending habits.

It may seem like a lot to do, but after you've filled out the log a few times it doesn't take long at all. The first time, I suggest you complete a log for each of the last three months. Although this first time it will probably take you a few hours, you'll find it to be a few hours well spent, because it will give you a baseline against which you can compare your expenses in the future. I'd then suggest you complete a log once a month for the next three months, allocating about an hour each month for this task. Then, when you're finished, you'll know how you've spent your money over a six-month period. And you'll have recorded enough data to determine your spending patterns. In fact, if you don't find it too difficult to do—and you probably won't—you might want to think about keeping a log for

FIGURE 5-1. THE LIFESTYLE LOG.

Expense	Amount
Monthly Fixed Expenses	
Housing	
Mortgage/Rent	$_____
Groceries	$_____
Utilities	$_____
Homeowner's/Renter's Insurance	$_____
Property Taxes	$_____
Transportation	
Car Loan/Lease Payments	$_____
Car Insurance	$_____
Gasoline	$_____
Maintenance/Repairs	$_____
Parking	$_____
Commuting	$_____
Health Care	
Health Insurance	$_____
Life Insurance	$_____
Doctor/Dentist Visits	$_____
Prescriptions/Medications	$_____
Disability Insurance	$_____
Child Care	
Day Care	$_____
Child Support	$_____
Total Fixed Expenses	**$_____**

Variable Expenses

Personal Care

Basic Grooming	$_____
Dry Cleaning/Wardrobe	$_____
Haircuts/Coloring	$_____

Home Maintenance

Repairs/Maintenance	$_____
Alarm/Pool Service	$_____
Lawn Care/Snow Removal	$_____
Cell Phone	$_____

Personal Enrichment

Adult Classes	$_____
Children's Activities	$_____
Health/Golf/Tennis Clubs	$_____
Hobbies	$_____
Gifts for Social Obligations	$_____
Travel for Social Obligations	$_____
Pet Care	$_____

Professional Services

Accountant	$_____
Attorney	$_____
Financial Adviser	$_____
Professional Dues	$_____

Miscellaneous

Vacations	$_____
Charitable Contributions	$_____
Banking/ATM Fees	$_____
Total Variable Expenses	**$_____**

(continues)

FIGURE 5-1. CONTINUED

Discretionary Expenses

Manicures/Massages	$_____
Cosmetics/Facials	$_____
Movies/Videos	$_____
Sporting Events/Art Exhibits/Performances	$_____
Baby-Sitting	$_____
Gambling	$_____
Restaurants/Bars	$_____
Takeout Food	$_____
"Toys" (e.g., jet skis, boat, Xbox)	$_____
Collecting (e.g., antiques, stamps)	$_____
Vacations	$_____
Other	$_____
Total Discretionary Expenses	**$_____**
Total Monthly Expenses	**$_____**

an additional nine months, rather than just three. Doing so would guarantee that you include all the seasonal expenses that you might otherwise miss.

The easiest way to start the Lifestyle Log is to go through your online bank account or checkbook and get the figures for your mortgage/rent payments, electric and/or oil bills, homeowner's/renter's insurance, and so forth, and then transfer them to the fixed expenses section. This part is usually pretty straightforward, since these expenses are typically your regular monthly bills. By the way, if you create the log as an Excel spreadsheet, you'll probably find it much easier to add everything.

Once that's done, you can move on to the variable and discretionary expenses. While you might find records of some of these expenses in your online bank account checkbook, you'll probably need to go back to your credit card and debit statements or online activity, too. In fact, the first time you fill out the log, you'll probably have to estimate some of these expenses that you used cash for and don't have a record of. Consequently, filling in this section may take some time. But tallying your variable and discretionary expenses is very important, because this is where the money flows—and where a lot of waste takes place.

After you've completed logs for the previous three months, it would probably be a good idea to start carrying around a small notebook so you can jot down all the little daily expenses that you wouldn't otherwise record. It's also a good idea to look at your transaction style to see if there isn't an easier, more efficient way to manage your money. If, for instance, you use multiple credit cards, you might want to cut down to only one or two. You'll get fewer statements, everything will be easier to track, and you'll save lots of time. It may come as a shock to you, but the average number of cards per household in the United States is 16.7—six bank cards, eight retail cards, and two or three credit cards. Imagine how much time people waste each month just keeping track of them. (Here's a time-saver: With your credit cards, you can download your monthly statements into planning software, which lets you group items by type of expense—it's a great tool.)

The Lifestyle Log works a lot like a successful shape-up plan. Once a friend and I were discussing our eating habits and he said, "I don't eat that much—three reasonable meals and hardly any snacks." A few weeks later he decided that he could use a little shaping up, and a trainer told him to start tracking his eating throughout the day. He soon discovered that those three reasonable meals weren't 2,500 calories but 3,000. Apparently, he had been overlooking the handful of M&Ms, the extra slice of pizza, and that second glass of Coke. Sure, he was famished, rushed, frazzled, or feeling down. He had plenty of reasons for consuming these extras. But it's only when he realized how much he had really been eating that he could start to do something about it.

The same thing happens with money. A lot of my clients tell me that even though they don't think they're spending a lot, their money seems to just disappear. It's what I think of as the Leaky Wallet Syndrome. A little here, a bit more there, and before you know it, there's nothing left.

LEAKY WALLET SYNDROME

In fact, one of the most important benefits of keeping the Lifestyle Log is that it helps you to fight Leaky Wallet Syndrome. After you've completed the log, you'll see that at least some, if not a lot, of your money is going to stuff that you really don't care about. Remember that time you went to Macy's to buy a couple of beach towels and came home not just with the towels, but also with four shirts from the sale rack, a birthday gift (wrapped for $10), and a new bottle of perfume? Or the time you went to the Land's End

website to check out a top for yourself and wound up buying new sweaters for the whole family? It's particularly easy
to spend a lot of money online; after all, since you don't
even have to sign for the purchase, it doesn't feel like you're
spending money. Not only that, the stores are open 24/7.

Because the log makes it possible for you to track these
expenses, it also makes it possible for you to avoid them.

The first year I completed the Lifestyle Log, I was
shocked to learn that my "leaky wallet" purchases were
clothes, restaurants, beauty products, and gifts. I'd been
spending a lot more on these items than I needed or, for
that matter, even *wanted* to spend—and I'd been completely unaware of it. But once I realized that these were
my trouble spots, I challenged myself to prioritize my
spending and bring down my expenses in these areas. And
I did it. Simply by becoming aware of how I was spending
my money, and being determined to do something about
it, I was able to decrease the amount I spent on clothes,
restaurants, and gifts. Although, I have to admit, the dollar
amount I spent on beauty actually increased, I was still able
to spend $100 less each month overall. And, most impor-
tant, I never felt deprived, because I was eliminating items
that I really didn't care about.

Being able to track your leaky wallet habits isn't the
only reason for you to keep a spending log. One of the log's
most important benefits is that it enables you to improve
your financial condition from quarter to quarter and year
to year. That's because keeping the log gives you both a
sense of accomplishment and a sense of purpose. It makes
you feel like you're doing something to get your spending

habits under control, which in turn makes you feel better about yourself and provides you with an impetus to make more improvements. In fact, once you've begun to change your spending habits and you've seen the results, you'll probably want to do even better, to beat your previous quarter's expenditures. And that desire to improve carries over from one year to the next.

Take out that three-ring binder you created earlier, as part of the exercises in Chapter Four to keep track of your earnings. Now, create separate tabs for "Checking Account" and "Credit Cards." Then, as you receive your monthly statements, file them in the binder so you can access them easily. If you manage any of your accounts online, print out a page of each month's transactions so that you have a paper record to go with the others.

Before you know it, you'll "find" the $500 a month to afford that house in the neighborhood you love. And if you continue to track your expenses over the course of a year, you'll get a good sense of your seasonal expenses as well as those expenses you incur all year. Just as our eating habits have seasonal cycles (think of all those pounds so many of us gain during the holidays or while on vacation), our spending runs in cycles. If you only summarize your expenses in January, how likely are you to remember the cost of having the lawn mowed in June? Or how much you'll have to spend on the kids for back-to-school supplies in September?

Keeping the Lifestyle Log is also beneficial because, once you've achieved control of your spending, when an unforeseen setback occurs—such as loss of your job, unexpected medical expenses, or parents who need help—you'll know immediately which funds you can redirect to cover your fixed expenses while taking care of those unanticipated expenses.

Let's say you lose your job. You have enough in your savings account to cover twelve months of living expenses. If you've kept a Lifestyle Log and know where your money goes, you can quickly figure out that you can save $150 a month by mowing your own lawn, reducing your takeout dinners to once every other week, and limiting manicures to once a month. Of course, an extra $150 a month isn't going to solve all your problems, but it will take away some of the stress of paying your monthly bills until you find a new job.

Finally, just in case you're still not sure that keeping the log is a good idea, let me remind you of the athlete's expression: "You gotta be in it to win it." That saying is just as true in managing your finances as it is in sports. Here's why: While researching this book, I conducted a number of focus groups made up of volunteers who said they were interested in learning more about handling their money. Their first assignment was always to complete a Lifestyle Log, after which we would discuss the results in the group. Typically, though, after two or three weeks, only half the people in each of the groups had actually done it. Since they all said they wanted to handle their money better, I was surprised that more people weren't willing to do something as simple as keeping a log.

What *didn't* surprise me, though, was that when the focus group was over, these same people felt they hadn't gotten as much out of it as those who had kept a log. Of course, they were more aware of their spending than they'd been before, but it was largely because they'd heard the insights of those who had kept track of their expenses.

For example, one woman who did the log was amazed how much she spent on many different kinds of vitamins. Someone who hadn't done the log needed to discover their own "trouble spot." I'm sure it's something, but probably *not* vitamins. In other words, in terms of your finances, "You gotta be in it to win it" means you have to be willing to take this first step toward getting a better grip on your spending. Until you find and measure your wallet's "leaks," you can't fix the problem.

SETTING GOALS

All right. Now that you've got a good idea of where your money is going, how do you use that information to get your finances in shape? You'll be happy to hear that one thing you *won't* be using the information for is to deprive yourself. Deprivation doesn't solve the problem. Taking buses instead of taxis didn't solve Carrie's problem, and it won't solve yours. Denying yourself things that are really important to you will only make you feel resentful and keep you from doing the Net Worth Workout.

The real solution to the problem is awareness: knowing where your paycheck and other income goes. Knowing about all the things—both large and small—you spend your money on. The Lifestyle Log gives you that awareness and helps you decide which of those things are important to you and which can go by the boards.

There are two ways you can use this information to improve your financial health. The first is to set goals for yourself; the second is to attain those goals.

Chapter Three discussed the importance of setting financial goals in general. Now I'm talking about *very specific* goals designed to bring down your fixed, variable, and/or discretionary expenses. But what kind of goals should you be setting?

When it comes to goals, there's no such thing as "one size fits all." Just as everyone's "trouble spot" isn't vitamins, there's no one goal that's right for everyone. You have to set goals that are right for *you*. This means that whatever goals you set should be based on your fixed, variable, and discretionary expenses, your Leaky Wallet Syndrome items, what you discovered about yourself from keeping the Lifestyle Log, and how much you can and/or want to cut back on your spending.

Still, there are a number of traits that all good goals have in common. One of the most important of these is specificity. You have to be very clear about what you want to achieve and when you want to achieve it. Just setting a goal of "lowering my mortgage payments" isn't enough. Instead, you should set a specific goal, such as "reducing my mortgage payments by $300 within the next six months." Don't just say, "I'll spend less at restaurants." Say instead, "I'll reduce the amount of money I spend eating out by 10 percent by the end of this month." Setting specific goals is essential because unless you know what you want to achieve, there's no way you can measure how close you've come to attaining it.

Whatever goal you set has to be a reasonable one. Let's say that you've decided to reduce your variable expenses by 50 percent in the next month. It would be great if you could do that. But odds are, you can't. If you set an unrealistic goal like that, and then find you can't attain it, you're likely to feel frustrated and disappointed. In fact, you may feel so frustrated and disappointed that you quit trying.

On the other hand, there's very little point in setting a goal that's extremely easy to reach—like spending $25 a month less. If it's that easy, it won't serve much purpose. Ideally, the goal should be one that makes you stretch somewhat, but not so much that you can never reach it. And if you're going to err, it's better to do so on the low side. Once you've achieved a lower goal, you can always set your sights higher.

Another important trait is comfort. As I said, one of the key elements of the Net Worth Workout is that you shouldn't deny yourself anything that's really important to you. Let's say, for instance, that you love to read. You typically buy and read a book every week. If you stopped buying books and started borrowing them from the library, you could probably save as much as $100 a month. But what if it's not just reading books but *owning* them that's important to you? You like keeping books on your shelves where you can see them and refer to them from time to time. In that case, it would be better for you to find somewhere else to save that $100. If the goal you set results in denying yourself something that's important to you, it will be difficult to attain, and attaining it won't bring you any satisfaction.

Make sure the goals you set are flexible. A lot of financial plans are too rigid. That's one reason so many of us avoid them—and why so many of them don't work. Imagine, for instance, you've set a goal of spending $200 less on your discretionary expenses this month. Then you discover that your favorite niece and her husband are coming to town. You'd like to take them out for dinner, but if you do, you won't be able to attain your goal. But what about that football game you were going to attend next week—are you willing to skip that instead? If so, you can take them out for dinner and still spend $200 less over the course of the month.

Finally, when you're setting goals, it's important that you take the long view. Don't get discouraged if you don't achieve your goals immediately. When I was sixteen, I had the lofty goal of finishing a marathon. Because I didn't know how to train, I didn't do enough long runs. Although I made it to the race, at mile twenty, I "hit the wall" and had to drop out. I was bitterly disappointed. But the experience of training had enriched my life. The long runs I did with my cross-country teammates, my faster times in short races, the fact that I was more alert and more productive in classes at school—all these things made my goal worth pursuing. And a year later, I crossed the same marathon's finish line with a respectable time. I've never looked back.

It's the same with financial goals. Let's say one of your goals is to cut your discretionary expenses by 20 percent next month. You cut out one restaurant meal a week, buy that outfit for the family wedding at a discount retailer, and use the ATM less. Even so, at the end of the month you discover that while your expenses have gone down, it's only by 15 percent. Of course you're disappointed—you only achieved three-quarters of your goal. On the other hand, you did spend 15 percent less on discretionary items than you did the month before. It may not be everything you hoped for, but it's a big step toward getting your finances in shape. And next month, if you also cut out betting in the office football pool (which you usually lose, anyway), you'll achieve that 20 percent reduction. You have to take the long view.

Regardless of the goals you set, the most important thing to remember about this whole process is that the purpose is to reduce spending and make use of that money to provide yourself with a financially secure future. So if you refinance your mortgage and find that you've saved $250 a month, it doesn't mean that you have an "extra" $250 to spend every month. If you do so, you're succumbing to the Spending Rule of Thumb—spending as much money as you make, and getting deeper and deeper into debt.

Whatever money you can keep from spending should be put into something that will be financially beneficial to you in the long term. That means saving or investing, which are two of the other financial quadrants of the Net Worth Workout. It's all interconnected, and it's the surest way to guarantee your long-term financial health.

Just to give you an idea of the way most people spend

their money, here are the percentages of after-tax income that the average American spends in each major category. These aren't necessarily recommendations for what you should be spending, but you can use these figures as benchmarks to measure your own expenses.

Housing	32%	Clothing	6%
Transportation	17%	Health Care	5%
Food	15%	Entertainment	5%
Insurance/Pension	9%	Other	3%
Education	8%		

After you've completed the Lifestyle Log, you're going to feel surprised, shocked, and probably guilty about some of your spending habits—the way dieters do upon realizing they've racked up extra calories. I recommend you address these trouble spots first, because once you do, you'll feel less stressed about your money. For instance, if after completing the log you realize that you spend more than you thought you did on lottery tickets and ATM fees, your goals could be to buy two lottery tickets this month instead of eight and to withdraw enough cash to cover yourself for a week, rather than having to go back to the bank every few days. I guarantee that if you make these small adjustments, you'll watch your cash more closely.

MEETING YOUR GOALS

All right, now that you've set your goals, how do you use the information in the Lifestyle Log to help you meet them? You can actually use the log to reduce your spending in all three areas, but it's probably best to start by looking at your discretionary and variable expenses. That's because, in any hierarchy of needs, they're the ones on the bottom, the ones that are least important and should be easiest to cut. Cutting them out is like cutting out the daily Krispy Kreme doughnuts and spring roll appetizers when you're dieting. They're easy to do without, and it helps you shed pounds quickly.

One of the best ways to reduce discretionary and variable expenses—particularly purchases that are made on impulse—is by using what I call the Spending Hangover Test. When you've had too much to drink you can have a hangover the next day. It's the same with spending: The day after you've spent too much money you can have a spending hangover. This kind of hangover may not leave you with a pounding headache or a queasy stomach, but it's a hangover just the same. You can tell that you've got one if you're feeling guilty the day after you've bought something that cost more than you're comfortable with. You know what I'm talking about. It's that expensive pair of boots, the dinner at that pricey restaurant, or the photograph for the living room wall that cost more than the couch and chairs put together.

Each of us has her own threshold. For one person, spending $50 on any variable or discretionary item might be enough to bring on a hangover; another person might be able to spend $500 before she begins to feel its effects. You have to determine what your threshold is, and once you do, make sure that you keep under it.

One of my clients, for instance, realized that her spending hangover threshold was $60, so she promised herself that she wouldn't spend that amount on any variable or discretionary item without giving it serious thought. One day, walking past a shop, she glanced into the window and saw a really cute sundress. She went in to look at the dress, promising herself that if it was priced above $60 she would walk away. It was $59. She bought it, and whenever she wears it she feels great, instead of feeling guilty for overspending.

Another client, Matt, promised himself that while purchasing furniture for his new home, he wouldn't buy anything on the spot if it cost more than $500. When he saw something he liked, he'd come back twenty-four hours later. If he still liked it, he bought it. Most of the time, though, he found he didn't even return to the store, deciding he wasn't that crazy about the piece, after all.

Another good way to reduce your discretionary and variable expenses is to look specifically for expenses that fall into one of two categories: convenience-driven expenditures (e.g., drive-through lunch, ATMs, bottled water, late video returns, and checkout-aisle magazines) and emotional buys (e.g., routine indulgences used to offset stress—manicures, cappuccinos, and gourmet takeout). Pay attention to these situations. It's only when you're aware that you're spending money you don't have to spend that you'll be able to avoid impulsive, convenience, and emotional spending.

Once again, make sure you distinguish between what's important to you and what you can do without. For one thing, when you deprive yourself of something you really want, you may end up spending more on a consolation prize. It's like the dieter who deprives herself of an ice cream cone only to stuff herself later with pizza and peanut butter. If you really want to treat yourself to that exotic plant for the garden, just forgo the impulse purchases—the magazines at the checkout counter and the protein shakes in the afternoon—long enough to save up for the plant. You'll be surprised how much better you'll feel when you do that instead of buying something the moment you see it and waking up the next day with a spending hangover.

In fact, there are lots of ways you can cut down on your discretionary and variable expenses and put that money to better use. Instead of spending $300 a month on restaurants and takeout food, one of my clients skipped one dinner out and put that $50 savings toward his son's education. Another client realized, after keeping the log for a couple of months, that he and his family were spending an enormous amount of money on junk food. Setting a goal to spend $100 less every month, they're putting the money aside for a long-awaited family trip to the Grand Canyon.

There are a number of ways to save on your variable expenses, too. Wear that suit an extra time before sending it to the dry cleaners. Go an extra week or two before coloring or cutting your hair. Instead of buying books (assuming you don't want to keep them), you can borrow them from the library or swap with your friends. Rather than buying an expensive gift, you can give your friend a nice frame with that picture of the two of you on vacation last summer. Just doing these things can easily give you another $75 a month toward your 401(k) contributions.

One of my clients, Carol, desperately wanted to buy an apartment, but she lacked the discipline to put aside enough for a down payment. Then she did the Lifestyle Log and discovered she was spending more than $1,000 a year on Bobbi Brown makeup. She promised herself that she wouldn't even walk into the department store until she'd put the money she was spending every month on cosmetics into a down payment account instead, along with the money she was saving by cutting out other expenses. Six months later, with a $500 balance, she went into the store, treated herself to a comparatively frugal $50 makeup purchase, and walked out.

You can use the information you've gathered in the Lifestyle Log to reduce your fixed expenses as well. In fact, it's just as easy to cut down on some of these expenses as it is in the other two areas. You can save on utilities by turning down the heat in the winter and the air conditioner in the summer. You can use coupons at the supermarket, use the self-serve pump when you buy gas, and have your teenager mow the lawn instead of paying someone else to do it. If you're willing to make more of an effort—and it would certainly be worthwhile—you can cut down on your fixed expenses even more by refinancing your mortgage, trading in your gas-guzzling SUV for a more economical car, or carpooling with neighbors instead of driving to work by yourself every day.

These are, of course, just some of the ways you can make use of the information in the log to reduce your expenses. In fact, one of the most interesting things about the Lifestyle Log is that everyone who uses it seems to find different ways to save money—and once they do, they usually change their behavior *immediately* so they can start saving. It's as if they can't resist. They get excited at the thought of putting that money to better use.

That's the secret to this program's success: You get to make positive changes in your behavior without having to give up anything that's really important to you. And the best thing about it is that what you don't spend winds up in the investing and saving quadrants, funding a better quality lifestyle in the future.

By following the Net Worth Workout, keeping a Lifestyle Log, reducing your expenses, and putting that money into investments or savings, you can provide yourself with enough money to live the way you want to. It's all about understanding the dynamics of personal finance—and the choices you make.

Remember, though, that with the Net Worth Workout, any progress is success. I really want you to achieve prosperity—if not outright wealth. But if you start diverting even as little as one percent of your spending to investing, that will be real progress, and it's important that you recognize that. In fact, that one positive change in your behavior will probably form the basis for even more positive changes in the future.

■   ■   ■

We've now covered the first two of the four quadrants of financial health—earning and spending. In the next chapter, I'll show you how to apply what you've learned by making smarter decisions in the first two quadrants to develop an easy and painless savings plan that will ensure your financial health—now and in the future.

NOTES

1. Tom Wolfe, *Bonfire of the Vanities.* (New York: Bantam, 1988).

2. Thomas J. Stanley, *The Millionaire Mind.* (Kansas City: Andrews McMeel Publishing, 2000) p. 299.

SAVING: HOW MUCH DO YOU SAVE IN A YEAR?

IF THE FIRST QUADRANT of financial health, earning, is like your metabolism, and the second, spending, is like what you choose to eat, the third quadrant, saving, is like strength training. It fortifies you and enables you to reach your goal. Let's say you're planning a bike trip to the Rockies. You'd probably want to build your strength by logging as much mileage as you could on your bike. You'd be sure to go to the gym for weight training, particularly working on your quadriceps. You'd also probably find a hill near your home and ride repeats to increase endurance. And to preserve your new muscle mass, you might add more protein to your diet.

Saving isn't any different. Financial strength training isn't just one type of activity, like opening a bank account with a higher interest rate. It's a whole set of behaviors. It's what you put into your retirement fund, and what your employer puts into it. It's what you set aside for major purchases such as furniture, a vacation, or a new car. It's planning for long-term goals like home ownership, a child's education, or retirement. And it's creating a three-to-six-month "safety net" in case you suddenly find yourself facing a short-term disability or job loss. It is sometimes the last thing you want to do, just like dragging yourself out of bed and getting to the gym can sometimes seem like the hardest thing you've ever done. But knowing it's an important thing to do, because it will help you in the long run, makes it easier. Saving allows you to build financial strength that will help you "stay the course" toward a stable, satisfying future. And because of that, it's a vitally important part of the Net Worth Workout.

Saving is a word that sometimes brings up unpleasant thoughts about denying ourselves the things we'd like to have, or even depriving ourselves of things we think we need. The fact is, though, that you can save money without feeling like a martyr. In this chapter I'll show you how to do just that by working on an easy and comfortable savings plan that will guarantee your financial health now and in the future.

WHY SAVING IS IMPORTANT

To increase your physical strength, you need to build muscle. Once you've developed that physical strength, you can draw on it to attain whatever long-, medium-, or short-terms goals you want. Increasing your financial strength—through saving—is no different. Short-term financial goals include such things as buying a new car or putting aside six months of living expenses in a savings account as a cushion. Medium-term goals might be taking a leave of absence from work, caring for elderly parents, or renovating your home. And long-term goals include education for your children, purchasing a home or business, or planning for a secure retirement for you and your spouse. With planning, all of these goals are attainable without disrupting your financial comfort today, just like a summit of the Rockies is attainable to a bicyclist with some perseverance.

Saving provides other very important benefits as well. I've found with my clients that it gives people peace of mind. It also strengthens their commitment to taking care of their finances, and the discipline they need to do it. Every time you increase the weights you use in the gym, you can feel yourself getting stronger. In the same way, every time you add another dollar to your savings or increase the percentage going to your 401(k), you feel empowered and financially stronger.

WHY SAVING IS SO DIFFICULT

If saving provides so many benefits, why is it so difficult? Maybe the most important reason is that the rewards for saving come only in the future, while spending money feels good immediately. To make it even more difficult, no one sees the fruits of your labor when you save. Your friends, family, colleagues, and neighbors can see you driving that snazzy new BMW, or they can come over to watch the Super Bowl on your fifty-six-inch TV. But if you choose to put more money into your brokerage account and continue driving your serviceable car and wait for your TV to wear out, they'll never see the $100,000 you've accumulated. You need to have confidence in knowing you've made the right decision by making your future secure.

Another reason many of us have so much trouble saving is that some of our saving behaviors have been shaped by watching our parents, older siblings, friends, and colleagues. We often unconsciously mimic their behaviors—financial and otherwise—just because it's what we're used to. Like most people's eating habits, exercise habits are shaped by their family. For example, when a client of mine tells me that he wants "safety" and "FDIC insurance," it usually turns out that his parents kept all their money in CDs and savings accounts. I'm here to help you recognize some of the habits you may be conditioned to and turn them into more productive ones.

The accounting firm Ernst & Young did a survey on why people are unable to save money. The three top reasons people gave were inflation, taxes, and procrastination. To some extent, of course, there's nothing we can do about either of the first two. Money does become less valuable over time. And death and paying taxes are, as the saying goes, the only two things we can be sure of. However, we can take steps to keep inflation and taxes from taking any more of a bite out of our income than they have to. As you read this chapter, I'll give you some concrete examples. In the meantime, one easy step we can all take to help us save money is to stop procrastinating.

Of course, if it was that easy to stop procrastinating, you would have done it already. The real reason so many of us procrastinate about saving money (or about doing anything we should, for that matter) is that we don't have a system in place. That's why the key to saving more money is to make it as automatic as possible. The best way to make sure you stay fit is to develop a fitness plan and stick to it, so it's a fixture in your day. You probably have noticed that the people you know who are most fit are the ones you see regularly in the gym or doing their early-morning walk. The same goes for saving—the less you have to think about it, the easier it will be.

Consider this: Most people end up with three to four major assets by the time they're sixty-five. Can you guess what they are? They're the equity in their homes, their 401(k)s, and/or their pension and Social Security payments. What do they all have in common? Procrastination isn't an option! They're what I'd call "low willpower savings techniques." If you don't pay your mortgage, you'll lose your house. When you sign up for a 401(k), your employer automatically deducts the money from your paycheck. If you work for a company long enough, it will usually pay you a pension when you retire. And of course the government takes money for Social Security along with your taxes. So making saving automatic and painless, with little effort on your part, is the best way to accumulate wealth.

First, let's figure out how much you've saved and set goals for how much you would like to save, then we will discuss ways to make saving more automatic and effortless.

FIGURING OUT HOW MUCH YOU'VE SAVED

As with all of the other financial health quadrants, the first exercise in this one is designed to help you figure out your current situation. That means answering the question: How much have I saved? And, as with the other quadrants, you can answer that question by doing an inventory. Take out the Net Worth Statement you put together in Chapter Three. Your savings will be everything listed under your assets that's liquid. That means your money market and saving accounts, mutual funds, stocks, bonds, IRAs, and 401(k)s.

If you didn't put together the Net Worth Statement previously, you can use the chart shown in Figure 6-1 to add up your savings. I do, though, strongly encourage you to do the statement—it's the backbone of the workout.

One of the benefits of this exercise is that it helps you target your saving "trouble areas," just like the Lifestyle Log helped you spot your spending trouble areas. When we're talking about physical fitness, many of us don't like our abdomens. Or maybe it's our triceps. Or we think our fannies are too well padded. When it comes to financial fitness, we also have to ask ourselves where we may need to focus our attention.

Where are we keeping our money? Is it in the best place? Can it be redistributed better? Let's say you've got most of your money in a savings account that's yielding 2 percent interest. And that instead of having the six months' worth of living expenses you should have, you've got eighteen months' worth of savings. Wouldn't it make more sense to put some of that money into an account that would provide

FIGURE 6-1.
ADD UP YOUR SAVINGS.

	Your Savings Inventory
Checking	$_____
Savings/Money Market	$_____
Mutual Funds	$_____
401(k)s	$_____
IRAs	$_____
Stocks/Bonds	$_____
Annuities	$_____
529 Plans	$_____
Custodial (UGMA/UTMA) Accounts	$_____
Restricted Stock	$_____
Options	$_____
Cash Value Life Insurance	$_____
Total	$_____

a return of more than 2 percent? Or to put it in a more tax-efficient vehicle like a Roth IRA?

Hoarding cash is an issue that comes up with my clients all the time. Some people are incredibly disciplined about saving money. Some of them even pinch pennies to do it! They avoid ATM fees by asking for "cash back" at the drugstore or grocery store. They always choose a higher deductible on their insurance to save money. And they request generic drugs when getting their prescriptions filled. Of course, these are all terrific money-saving activities. But then some people take all that money they've saved and put it into a low-yielding savings account! It's like putting in a lot of hard work at the gym only to eat nothing but junk food the rest of the time! You're just wasting all that good effort.

DECIDING HOW MUCH YOU SHOULD SAVE

When I tell my clients how important it is for them to save money, the question they always ask is, "How much should I save?" And I always answer, "As much as you can afford." The fact is that the more you save, the better off you'll be down the line. As I said, though, you don't have to deprive yourself of things that are important to you in order to save. And you certainly shouldn't skimp on things you need. Having money in the bank is great, but not if you feel like you can't treat yourself to a nice dinner.

Generally speaking, I think that a good goal is to be saving 10 percent of your gross income by the time you're thirty years old. Remember, gross income is your total income before taxes, health insurance, and other expenses are taken out. So, if you earn $50,000 a year, your after-tax income may be $32,500. But I'm recommending that you save $5,000 a year, not $3,250.

If you're a woman, I'd suggest you shoot for 12 percent, because women tend to earn less, live longer, and pay more for products and services like haircuts and dry cleaning. We're also typically out of the workforce for eleven years while raising children, which limits our earning power. If you need a frame of reference for the difference that saving a higher percentage makes, you can think of it this way. If 5 percent is scraping by, then 10 percent is managing, 15 percent is terrific, and 20 percent is fantastic.

Incidentally, when I say 10 percent (or 12 percent), I'm not including whatever your company may match for your 401(k) plan. Because the company match is "free money" from an outside source, it's not really coming from you. Including it would be like letting your trainer haul your weights and then bragging to friends, "Benched 100 today!" Besides, it's best to use the company's match as part of your total savings "cushion."

In addition, a very important "savings cushion" everyone should have is between three and six months' worth of living expenses in a savings, money market, CD, or other easily accessible account. (Hopefully, you've completed your Lifestyle Log so you know what those living expenses really are.) If you're self-employed or work in a particularly volatile industry, I would recommend that you put aside as much as a year's worth of living expenses.

It's true, unfortunately, that money in accounts like these doesn't work very hard for you. But it does have the advantage of instant liquidity. If something goes wrong—you lose your job, the roof leaks, or your car breaks down—or even if you just want to splurge on a great vacation, the money will be there and you can get at it easily without paying astronomical rates on your credit cards. The tradeoff in low returns is more than offset by the costs you'd incur if you had to borrow using your credit cards or (the worst option of all) your 401(k), or had to sell stocks or bonds at a loss.

If you need further motivation for saving more, train

yourself to think of it this way. Because of inflation, $1 spent today means forgoing $6.07 in the future. (That's assuming you invest the dollar in an account that earns 10 percent for twenty years, at a 3 percent inflation rate.) So when you're thinking about buying something, ask yourself if you'll get $6.07 worth of use for every dollar you're going to spend on it. I was explaining this very point one day to my client Mike, who was sitting in my office drinking a bottle of Poland Spring for which he'd just paid a dollar. Pointing to the bottle, I said, "What do you think?" And he said, "I think I should start drinking from the water cooler." Sometimes it's as simple as that to start taking steps to save!

DEVELOPING A SAVINGS PLAN

In the long run, the best way to save money is to develop a plan—that is, establish a routine—for doing it. If you want to get physically fit, you might hire a trainer to motivate you to go to the gym. You also might agree to meet a friend every Monday, Wednesday, and Friday to walk together. Or you might join a gym that you can go to straight from work. I sign up for April and May races in January because it forces me to prepare for them during the winter. In other words, you develop a routine, something automatic, that you can follow easily.

Developing a plan to save money works the same way. Earlier I explained how most of us already have a way to build up assets using three automatic plans: home owner-ship, 401(k) accounts, and pension and/or Social Security benefits. Let's look at how you can get the most out of your plans.

First, and probably the easiest way, is to have money taken directly out of your paycheck, before temptation can strike. What makes this option even more attractive is that having money deducted automatically also saves you on payroll taxes if it's going to a retirement account. Uncle Sam *wants* you to save and has rigged the tax code to help you do it through 401(k)s, IRAs, and SEPs if you're self-employed.

The best savings plan I know is one called Save More Tomorrow, which was developed by Richard Thaler at the University of Chicago. All you have to do is commit in advance to saving a portion of whatever salary increases you may get in the future. Believe me, the results are astounding! In a recent test, people who followed this plan found that their average savings rate increased from 3.5 percent to 11.6 percent over twenty-eight months! And it's easy to do yourself.

This is how it works. Let's say you've just learned you're about to get a 4 percent increase in your salary. Of course, it would be nice to have all that extra money. But since you're not used to having it anyway, putting some of it aside shouldn't be a problem. What you do, then, is go to your benefits web page or call your human resources department and ask them to increase your 401(k) contribution by 2 percent. It's very important, though, that you increase your contribution rate *before* you actually receive the 4 percent increase in your paycheck. If you wait until you see all the money in one check, and then see some of it gone in the next, you may feel deprived.

Another good way to save is to direct a certain amount of your paycheck to an account that you can't readily access. But be sure to challenge yourself! My client Mike participated in a plan that took $10 out of every paycheck to put toward buying savings bonds, which he did for seven years. It was a great way to save money, but it wasn't as great as it could have been. Although Mike's income increased by $30,000 over seven years, he never increased the amount that was taken out for savings. Think of how much more he could have saved if his savings had kept up with his income! That's why the Save More Tomorrow approach will fortify your savings much faster.

As you can see from all these examples, planning doesn't have to be an exhaustive process. Reading this book and implementing the Net Worth Workout is a way of planning. So is attending a seminar on financial planning. Even talking with friends about your financial plans can help. The point is that even people who have planned a little will have a good deal more money than those who haven't planned at all! On the other hand, planning to save is very much like saving itself—the more you do it, the better off you'll be.

DECIDING WHICH SAVINGS VEHICLE IS BEST FOR YOU

Now that you've got a plan for saving money, the obvious question is, "Where do I put all the money I'm saving?" There are several possibilities. You can use financial products such as savings accounts, CDs, and money markets, or investments like stocks and bonds. However, before you decide which product to use, let's understand the vehicles you can use that will help you maximize what you save by providing you with special tax incentives, such as IRAs, 401(k)s, and pension plans; college 529 plans; UGMA/ UTMA accounts; and Coverdell education savings accounts.

But depending on what you're saving for, some of these vehicles are better than others. What I'm going to do, then, is tell you a little bit about each one, and then tell you more in Chapter 7 on investments. The most important thing to remember is that you should align your savings equipment with goals. If you wanted to tone your arms, would you then go into a gym and use a leg press? Or attempt to improve your flexibility by taking up golf instead of yoga? It sounds obvious, but it happens more than you would think. Too often, low-yielding CDs are used for retirement accounts and savings bonds are used for junior's college fund. If you know the right equipment to use, you're most likely to see the best results!

Savings Accounts

Savings accounts are, of course, the traditional place to put your money. It's where your grandparents, great-grandparents, and probably even great-great-grandparents put the money they saved so it could accrue interest. The greatest advantages that savings accounts offer are safety and liquidity. That is, you don't have to worry about losing your money—at least as long as the bank stays in business. And you can get to the money easily when you need it. But savings accounts also have one big disadvantage—they don't shelter you from taxes and inflation, the investor's chief danger. Here's why.

Let's say you have $20,000 earning 2 percent in a savings account, and you're in the 30 percent tax bracket. If you earn $400 in interest, you have to pay taxes of $120. That means that you've really only earned $280. "Okay," you may say, "I can live with that." But then you have to take inflation into account. If inflation is running, say, at 3 percent a year, which it typically does, $600 of your savings account will be lost to inflation every year. This means that once you factor in taxes and inflation, not only has the value of your savings account not increased by $400, it's actually lost $320 after accounting for taxes and inflation. That's why savings accounts are best when you're putting away money that you expect to use in the not-too-distant future.

Certificates of Deposit (CDs)

A certificate of deposit is a time deposit with a bank. CDs are not completely liquid like a savings or checking account. They have a specific maturity date (from three months to five years) and a specified interest rate. If you need the money before the maturity date you're subject to a penalty. CDs provide safety and are insured by the Federal Deposit Insurance Corporation (FDIC), but the interest is taxed at your ordinary income tax rate. CD rates are usually low, like savings accounts, but they can pay a bit more because you are locking your money up with the bank.

Money Market Accounts

A money market is a fund that invests in short-term debt instruments. The fund's objective is to earn interest for you while maintaining a net asset value of $1.00 per share. This type of fund is safe, but expected income from it is low. You can also purchase money market funds that have tax-free yields. The best use of these funds, like savings accounts and certificates of deposit, is to provide liquidity and safety for your short-term needs.

Individual Retirement Accounts (IRAs), 401(k)s, and Pension Plans

The most widely recognized savings vehicles for getting your financial muscles in shape are retirement plans, including IRAs, 401(k)s, and pension and other plans. Of course, 401(k)s and pension plans are only available through your employer. IRAs are available at most major financial institutions, such as banks, brokerage firms, mutual fund companies, or insurance companies.

You'll learn more about all of these retirement plans in the next chapter, but for now, let's take a quick look at what they can accomplish. The greatest benefit of these programs is that they can reduce your taxes today (the Roth IRA being an exception) and while they're earning money because all your contributions are before tax. You pay the taxes when you withdraw from these accounts in your retirement. You make the contributions and your employer may match some of these contributions. If you contribute $10,000 to a 401(k) plan and earned $60,000 that year, your adjusted gross income is reduced to $50,000. You only owe taxes on $50,000, not the $60,000 you earned. When you withdraw the contributions from your 401(k) during your retirement, then you'll pay taxes. But while your account is growing, all your money grows tax deferred.

Traditional IRAs also reduce your taxes. However, if you contribute to a retirement plan at work and earn over $32,000 if you're single and $52,000 if you're married filing jointly, then you won't be able to fully deduct your IRA. If you don't have a retirement plan at work, you can deduct up to $4,000 if you're single and $8,000 if you're married filing jointly.

Another type of IRA is a Roth IRA. Although Roth IRAs don't reduce your income taxes today, they can save you a boatload in the future. Let's say you saved $4,000 a year in a Roth IRA for thirty years and earned 10 percent. That means you personally saved $120,000, which is quite a lot of money. After thirty years, though, you've actually got $650,000, and you can withdraw as much or as little of that money as you want—and tax-free! If, say, you were to withdraw 4 percent each year, you'd have a tax-free stream of income of over $2,100 a month. Not a bad savings plan!

Finally, pension plans or defined-benefit plans work differently still. Traditionally, your employer makes contributions on your behalf. Depending on the plan employers offer, when you retire they will either allow you to roll over a lump sum (also known as a cash balance pension plan) to an IRA or offer you the option to annuitize your account. This is called an annuity, where you receive a fixed amount each month based on your age and the value of your account. You don't have discretion to invest like you can in a 401(k). However, there isn't any investment risk and you can receive guaranteed lifetime income. The participant is usually not required to make contributions, but it's possible.

College 529 Plans

These plans are the fastest-growing option for people interested in saving for their children's education, for good reason. They allow you to contribute up to $11,000 per parent, per child, each year, with a cumulative maximum contribution of over $250,000. Even better, these funds grow tax-deferred, which means you don't pay any taxes while the funds remain in a 529 plan, and when you withdraw them to pay college expenses, they're federal tax-free. The funds are tax-free in some states as well, and some states give deductions for contributions to their section 529 plan. The downside is that if you withdraw the money to buy yourself a boat instead of paying for your kids' schooling, you pay income taxes and a penalty of 10 percent. However, if the hard work of one of your kids pays off and he earns a full ride, you can change the account to another beneficiary, even yourself, should you decide go to cooking school or get that masters degree you always wanted!

Coverdell Education Savings Accounts

Coverdell education savings accounts (ESAs) let you make annual nondeduction contributions. Your account grows free of federal income taxes and your withdrawals can be tax-free, too. Unlike the 529 plan, the funds can also be used for elementary and secondary school expenses. The contributions have a $2,000 limit per year. Also, your contribution eligibility is based on adjusted gross income of $95,000 to $110,000 for singles or $190,000 to $220,000 for married couples filing joint tax returns.

UGMA and UTMA Accounts

The primary purpose of these accounts is to have an easy way to make gifts of money and securities to minors. (They are named for laws adopted by most states—UGMA for the Uniform Gift to Minors Act; UTMA for the Uniform Transfer to Minors Act.) The accounts are under the control of a custodian, typically a parent or relative, until the child is an adult. The child can take control of these funds as young as age 18 or up to age 21, depending on the state. The custodian makes the decisions about buying, selling, reinvesting earnings, and so on. The custodian may also withdraw the money to spend for the benefit of the child. If the child is under age 14, the income from this account is taxed to the child up to a relatively low amount and then it can be taxed at the parent's rate.

Parents have used UGMA/UTMA funds to provide gift funds to their children without being subject to gift taxes (for 2005, the annual gift tax exclusion is $11,000). The problem with these accounts, though, is that you can't take the money back. These assets belong to your child. If the minor, upon reaching the age of majority, decides to go to Tahiti instead of college, legally the money is your child's to do with as he chooses.

■ ■ ■

As you can see, depending on what you're planning to use the money for, and when you're planning to use it, some options are better than others. The important thing for you to remember is that if you take these issues into account when you make the decision about which savings vehicle is best for you, you'll be sure to be making the most of the money you've put aside.

COORDINATING SAVING WITH THE OTHER QUADRANTS

If you work out consistently, the more strength you build up, the more benefits you'll receive. A hard-body, for example, can enjoy a New York sirloin guilt-free or snack on a peanut-butter-and-jelly sandwich. That's because strong muscles burn fat calories more efficiently. Making that extra strength-training effort also enables you to work out better—and have more endorphins flowing—and yet you won't experience as much stiffness the next day as you'd feel if you weren't as strong. In other words, building up physical strength today gives you additional strength that you can use in the future.

Building financial strength works exactly the same way. Decreasing your spending and increasing your savings today lets you build up your financial strength so you'll have more money to spend tomorrow. The fun part is that it means you'll be able to buy that larger house, if you wish, take more expensive vacations, or even drive a fancier car. It also means that you'll be able to be more generous to the people you care about, as well as to whatever causes you may wish to support.

This exercise, which I do with my clients, should give you a pretty good idea of what I'm talking about. I call it the Winner vs. the Loser exercise. Here's how it works.

Let's assume there are two people—Sam the Spender and Susie the Saver. Each starts off with an annual salary of $40,000, begins working at age 21, and retires at age 65. Sam the Spender saves 5 percent of his income every year, while Susie the Saver saves 20 percent of hers. In the first year, on his $40,000 salary, Sam the Spender will save $2,000 and have $38,000 to spend. Susie the Saver will save $8,000 and have $32,000 to spend.

They both invest their savings in an S&P 500 mutual fund that averages 10 percent a year. After the first year, Sam's income has grown to $40,200—that is, $40,000 plus the 10 percent return on his $2,000. Susie's income is now $40,800—$40,000 plus the 10 percent return on her $8,000 investment. They both have more to spend since their investments have produced yields. Maintaining the same percentages, the next year Sam spends $38,190 and saves $2,010, while Susie spends $32,640 and saves $8,160. As the years pass, Sam continues to save just 5 percent of his income and Susie 20 percent. Eighteen years later, Sam has an income of $41,802 a year and Susie has $49,065. Not much of a difference there, except Susie now has more to spend every year (see Figure 6-2).

By the time both Susie and Sam reach age 65, the difference is considerably greater. Sam's income is $49,065 while Susie's is $69,271—more than $20,000 a year more. Even more important is the difference in their investment portfolios. By saving 5 percent a year Sam will have accumulated $121,000. Susie, saving 20 percent, will have accumulated more than $483,000! Sure, Sam the Spender had an advantage for a short while. But before long, Susie the Saver came out—and stayed—ahead. Saving more money every year actually gave Susie another advantage as well. Thanks to this extra income, her lifestyle was substantially less harried and less stressful. She could now afford things that made her life easier, such as frequent trips and the chance to eat out more often.

As you can see from these examples, the more you save,

FIGURE 6-2. THE WINNER VS. THE LOSER EXERCISE

	Susie the Saver			Sam the Spender		
Age	Income	Saves	Spends	Income	Saves	Spends
21	$40,000	$8,000	$32,000	$40,000	$2,000	$38,000
22	$40,800	$8,160	$32,640	$40,200	$2,010	$38,190
39	$49,065	$9,813	$39,252	$41,082	$2,054	$39,028
65	$69,271	$13,854	$55,417	$49,065	$2,453	$46,612

the more of a difference it makes. But it's important to re-member that saving is only part of the story, only one of the four financial health quadrants of the Net Worth Work-out. It impacts, and is impacted by, the other three quad-rants. In Chapter Four, you learned that earnings aren't just your paycheck, but include many other sources of income, and that chances are you are bringing in more money than you realized. In Chapter Five on spending, you got a clearer idea of how much money was going out, and proba-bly discovered that it was more than you'd thought! You also learned that when you control your spending it allows you to save more. In this chapter you've seen how those savings can provide you with financial muscle for the future. Chapter 7, on investing, will show you how to make the most of your hard work from savings and how coordinating all four quadrants—earning, spending, saving, and invest-ing—will allow you to provide yourself with the kind of financial security you've always wanted.

INVESTING: WHAT SHAPE ARE YOUR INVESTMENTS IN?

THERE'S A SPECIAL REASON investing is the Net Worth Workout's last quadrant. Investing completes the circle of the four quadrants and drives synergy throughout. Investing delivers peak performance: future income with minimal taxes. Any change here contributes more to your prosperity, dollar for dollar, than a change to another quadrant. Smart investing gives you the rewards of portfolio income—dividends, interest, and capital gains—discussed in Chapter 4.

Investing is about building a foundation for today and the future, and it is a lot like cardiovascular training. Cardiovascular work boosts your heart and respiration rates and, as a result, your capacity. A strong heart holds down your "real age" and turbocharges energy and wellness. Similarly, investing ultimately drives your wealth. No other quadrant in the Net Worth Workout has this great an impact. Just using your current paycheck sensibly won't do it. You need a measure of intensity.

This effort also needs to span various areas. If you're serious about fitness, you don't just work your heart and lungs; you mix it up. An investment portfolio does the same thing. Even better, a properly aligned portfolio can protect you from the pain of taxes and fluctuations in the market.

Our first exercise, the Investment Inventory, shows you exactly what you own, whether as a solo individual or as someone in a formal relationship. Then we'll tackle five capacity-building drills. This is the heart of your investment workout. These drills are designed to help you get the most out of the investments you have. The chapter closes with a special section on women and investing.

THE INVESTMENT INVENTORY

Let's start with you, the center of it all. It's important to look at your investments in the aggregate. Remember, your portfolio is just a part of your holdings. Plus, your investments may be just one half of a larger portfolio. Are you married, or the legal or emotional equivalent? If so, do you think of "your" investments collectively?

Please don't feel bad if you don't. Most households divide their chores, so finances usually fall to one person. But in this day and age, the old model leaves many of us in the lurch—not to mention that it leaves many of us with portfolios that don't do as well as they're capable of. As my dad says, "No one of us is as smart as all of us."

Most people come to see me asking what to buy, rather than thinking of the big picture. It's like a runner who thinks a certain pair of shoes or having perfect weather conditions will determine his performance. They can help, but they're not the determining factor. Let's take a step back and first complete the Investment Inventory shown in Figure 7-1. What investments do you have? Include retirement accounts, brokerage accounts, annuities, and savings beyond your three-to-six-month emergency reserve. Also, what is your annual return in each of these accounts? You can find the rate of return on your investments by looking them up on Morningstar.com.

If you had $50,000 in your 401(k) and $30,000 in an IRA, and the 401(k) earned 8 percent interest last year and the IRA earned 12 percent interest last year, then weighting it by account size, your annual return would be 9.5 percent (0.08 x $50,000 + 0.12 x $30,000 = $7,600/$80,000).

How well are your investments serving you? What do you need from your investments? Not asking those questions is tantamount to pushing off the top of a ski slope with no sense of the terrain and people below. You want to enjoy the ride. And to do that, you need to gauge your level of physical exertion, which in terms of your investment portfolio means knowing the most risk you feel you should tolerate.

FIGURE 7-1. COMPLETE AN INVESTMENT INVENTORY.

	Your Investment Inventory	1-Year Annual Return	3-Year Annual Return
Mutual Funds	$_____	_____	_____
401(k)s	$_____	_____	_____
IRAs	$_____	_____	_____
Pension Plans	$_____	_____	_____
Stocks	$_____	_____	_____
Bonds	$_____	_____	_____
Annuities	$_____	_____	_____
529 Plans	$_____	_____	_____
UGMA/UTMA Accounts	$_____	_____	_____
Cash-Value Life Insurance	$_____	_____	_____
Stock Options	$_____	_____	_____
Restricted Stock	$_____	_____	_____
Total	**$**_____	_____	_____

Think of an espresso and how it makes you feel. What a buzz! It definitely boosts your heart rate. But investments can resemble espresso, too: Some of them may give your portfolio a quick boost but do nothing for your long-term well-being. Similarly, being too conservative is also a mistake. Investments are not made to just sit there. Ideally, each dollar should launch others over time. Apples to more apples, as it were. That's what compounding is about.

FIVE CAPACITY-BUILDING DRILLS

Now let's talk exercise physiology for a minute. In a cardio-vascular workout, your heart and lungs drive oxygen-rich blood at peak capacity. By exercising hard and sustaining it, you maximize your workout. This is where progress happens. And the stronger your heart and lungs grow, the farther you can push your training capacity. Every system of the body thrives with optimal conditioning: Muscles gain mass and definition, capillaries branch out further into adjoining tissue, and so on. All your systems function in synergy.

When it comes to investing, you'll do well to master five capacity-building drills. They are compounding interest, dollar-cost averaging, tax reduction, tax deferral, and diversification. It's exactly like cross-training: Relying on some of each gives you better performance than relying on one or two.

Compounding Interest

Albert Einstein famously quipped, "The most powerful force in the universe is compound interest." He was right—investments build empires. Of course, we all live with constraints, such as major developments in the nation's economy. But even so, our investments should stand the test of time.

We also have more time than we think. If you start working at age 22 and live until age 83, that's sixty-one years. Even if you're forty-three years old today, you still face another forty years of compound interest. As I tell my clients, that's a great opportunity—and way too many days to worry and wonder, "How did the market do today?" Remember, without compounding interest in your portfolio, you're like an athlete who drinks espresso to energize himself for the next Olympics.

Here's one example of the power of compound interest. Say that, starting in 1960, your mom put $1,000 a year into the S&P 500 for the next forty-four years. With its average rate of return of 10 percent, she'd have had $717,905 in 2004. Investing that $44,000 over those forty-four years delivered substantial returns. What's especially striking about Mom's happy outcome, though, is its growth curve. At her twenty-two-year mark in 1982, your mom's then-$22,000 investment would have been worth just over $78,000—a tidy $56,000 profit. Not bad, I'll grant you.

But the real magic would have occurred in the next twenty-two years. Grand finale: Mom's $78,542, plus her annual $1,000 addition, would have ballooned. Think of it: She added the same $22,000 but her account grew from $78,542 to $717,905. The magic of compounding created almost $640,000 more during the same amount of time! Go, Mom!

Also, as any good financial coach will tell you, growing your holdings from $10,000 to $100,000 is psychologically much tougher than going from $100,000 to $1 million. En route to $100,000 you're apt to feel doubts, especially if things go awry. You're apt to ruminate, "I've lost $5,000.

What's the point?" You're hardly alone in such doubts, even if far smaller sums are involved. In fact, behavioral economists have coined a term for it: "the loss-aversion effect." The dismay of loss is two and a half times more intense than the pleasure of winning. Yet loss aversion prevents us from winning in the long run.

Still, seasoned investors on their way to $1 million in assets have learned to tolerate the short-term losses and uncertainty each year to average 10 percent in the stock market instead of a 3 percent guarantee in their savings. They develop confidence that they can succeed. It's much like an athlete's willingness to work through discomfort or inconvenience.

To extend our cardiovascular metaphor, it takes time to build a strong body. And much of that progress comes "once you get rolling." For instance, a rookie's system doesn't rev nearly as high as a seasoned athlete's. It's understandable that rookies grow impatient. Anyone who makes a big initial effort at training can get discouraged: Their performance (e.g., their time to run a mile) will be nothing like a veteran's. Here's where savvy coaches prove invaluable: They manage expectations, reassuring the rookie that setbacks and slow times are perfectly normal.

Dollar-Cost Averaging

Let's move on to the next capacity-building drill: dollar-cost averaging.

Dollar-cost averaging is one of the best investing habits you can build. It's not unlike the habit of working out reg-

ularly. Plus it's a cinch to do. Instead of investing your
assets in a lump sum, you work your way into buying funds
by buying smaller amounts over a longer period of time.
You buy a certain amount of your investment on a regular
schedule regardless of the market. More shares are bought
when prices are low and fewer shares are bought when
prices are high.

The Dollar-Cost Averaging Exercise

One of the happiest surprises of the past decade's physical fitness research was that someone who exercises moderately each
day, for twenty minutes or so, often winds up in better shape
than someone who exercises hard once or twice a week. This
dovetails nicely with the Save More Tomorrow practice (see
Chapter Six), where you promise a set percentage of any pay
raise to a defined-contribution plan. Without the dollar-cost averaging that a defined contribution permits, investors couldn't hit
their target.

The beauty of dollar-cost averaging is twofold. It often holds
down your average cost per share, and it disciplines you to invest. The standard annual investment, which I recommend, is 10
percent of your gross income by the time you're thirty years old.
If you're older and are getting a late start, increase this percentage to the highest you can afford.

Spend a fixed amount on investing in mutual funds per
month. Without even trying, you automatically buy more shares
when prices are low and fewer shares when they rise in price.

You scoop up bargains, many of which may turn into winners. And you won't get overzealous about every hot stock.

The table below shows how dollar-cost averaging works over a six-month period with the person usually buying shares in a mutual fund, most often in his 401(k) or company retirement plan.

Routine Investment	Price per Share	Shares Purchased
$500	$10	50.00
$500	$11	45.45
$500	$ 8	62.50
$500	$ 7	71.42
$500	$ 9	55.55
$500	$11	45.45
Average	$ 9.08	

In this example, your total investment for six months was $3,000, and you bought 330.37 shares. So your share price (i.e., "dollar cost") averaged out at $9.08. Had you bought the same number of shares at an average of $11 each when the market was high, you'd have paid $634 more. Two more terrific benefits relate to freedom—freedom from the effort and from the stress of deciding whether "now is the time to invest."

Making your monthly investing workout a way of life helps in less obvious ways, too. The natural inclination of novice investors is to go with whatever's doing well at the moment. They usually invest large lump sums because of a trigger event—they receive an inheritance, have a 401(k) to roll over, change jobs, or sell a home and aren't buying a new one.

That's hardly a brilliant tactic, either. You want to "practice" by investing smaller amounts. This way, when the big race comes up, you've already made your mistakes during workouts; there's less pressure; plus you're less apt to get psyched out. For instance, in a bull market, many share prices can be inflated beyond their true worth. Conversely, even in a weak market, many "bargains" are clunkers. So take it from a seasoned investor: Buy methodically using dollar-cost averaging.

Most important, remember that if you are trying to time the market, you'll face a lot of stress and risk. With any investment, you have to be right twice: when you buy and when you sell. And typically, the more often you trade, the lower your average return. It's a classic paradox: People are often unjustifiably overconfident in assessing their abilities and knowledge about the world around them. Like most car drivers, most investors think they're above average.

Economists know it better than anyone. They devote a considerable amount of time to the public's undue optimism and overconfidence. According to Gary Belsky and Thomas Gilovich in *Why Smart People Make Big Money Mistakes,* "Even when people know as much as they think they know, it's often not as much as they need to know."[1]

Here is a sobering stat. According to research firm Dalbar, over the past nineteen years the average equity investor earned 2.57 percent annually, compared to 12.22 percent for the S&P 500 Index. Alas, many investors exhibit counterproductive tendencies. For instance, they sell their best holdings "before they lose value," and "wait" for their weak stocks to appreciate.

If you had just missed the best five days in the ten-year period ending December 31, 2003, it would have cost you $6,469 in potential earnings on a $10,000 investment of stocks that make up the S&P 500. Missing the top-twenty days was even worse. Your return would have dropped from a compound annualized return of 11.06 percent to 2.06 percent!

Remember, it's time *in the market* that matters, not timing the market. So I urge you to avoid these traps. Pace yourself and commit to investing for the long run.

Tax Reduction

My third piece of advice is this: Invest in a way that shrinks your taxable income. You can do so through robust and constant participation in retirement plans. The tax code gives you several options; make the most of whatever fits your case.

Employees are typically eligible for a 401(k), 403(b), employee stock ownership plan (ESOP), or a traditional IRA. Self-employed people can direct their retirement funds to simplified employee pension (SEP) IRAs and profit-sharing plans, where contributing may be even more favorable.

"Defined contribution" is IRS-speak for "preset performance goals for a workout year." Do you want to boost your reps on the weights circuit or drop ten pounds? Just figure out what amount you want withheld from each paycheck and send it to investments. Any defined-contribution plan constitutes a tax shelter, being income your employer detours for you before Uncle Sam can size up your tax hit.

Until age 49, you can stash up to $15,000 of a 401(k) or 403(b) or 457 plan per year. At age 50 and beyond, you can use a "catch up" provision that allows an additional

$5,000 for a total of $20,000. Best of all, reducing your taxable income by $15,000 really helps in two ways. Let's imagine you make $100,000 a year with no 401(k). You'll pay 31 percent in taxes, or $31,000. Steer that $15,000 to a 401(k), and your income "drops" to $85,000; accordingly, your tax burden falls to $26,350—saving you 15 percent, or $4,650, in taxes this year.

Contribution Limits for 401(k), 403(b), and 457 Plans

Year	Maximum Allowable (Age 49 and Under)	Catch Up (Age 50 +)
2006	$15,000	$20,000
2007 and beyond	Limits are indexed in $500 increments for inflation.	

Now let's sweeten this deal. The bulk of American retirement accounts are 401(k)s, where you personally control your investment choices. Typically, an employer matches a percentage of your 401(k) investment; 5 percent is the norm. Say your employer offers a match, too. Together you're investing $20,000 toward retirement this year alone—20 percent of your annual income! And don't forget, for now you're saving $4,650 in taxes, money you can invest to lessen the impact of your future tax burden.

Imagine now that you discipline yourself to make our financial-style "cardiovascular training" a way of life. Say you're forty-four years old now. Start by investing $15,000 in a new defined-contribution plan.

Hypothetically, your employer matches it with $5,000,

for a total deposit of $20,000 this year. By the time you're sixty-six, if you add $20,000 each year and average 10 percent annual return, that would bring your retirement account to a level of $1,408,055.

It gets better if you want to share your knowledge with the next generation. Imagine that you're teaching this equation to your twenty-two-year-old who's just landed his first "career" job. At first, his contributions will be lower, but we can also expect that the maximum contribution will increase above $15,000 a year for him, if he contributes on average $20,000 a year. When he's sixty-six, his retirement account will hold $14,358,097—enough to take very good care of his loving, financially savvy parents.

Individual Retirement Accounts: Another Way to Reduce Taxes

For years, people have turned to IRAs to fund their retirements. The upside is they're available to you when other vehicles aren't. The downside is that your contribution *is capped low:* the lesser amount of your earned income versus $4,000 (taxpayers age 50 and over are permitted an extra "catch-up contribution" of $1,000). Even if your spouse isn't earning an income, you can add up to $4,000 on his or her behalf.

Roth IRAs are the newest addition to your workout bag. Congress created them in the Economic Growth and Tax Relief Reconciliation Act of 2001. A single taxpayer whose adjusted gross income (AGI) is $95,000 or less ($150,000 for married couples) can contribute up to $4,000 annually. (If you're fifty years old or over, there is a $1,000 catch-up provision. In 2008, these contribution limits increase to $5,000 if you are age 49 and under, and $6,000 if you're age 50 or over.)

Alternatively, you can make a "phased-out contribution." In that case if you're single, your AGI can range between $95,000 and $110,000. Your contribution limit is reduced when your AGI reaches $95,000, and eliminated entirely when your modified AGI reaches $110,000. Correspondingly, for married couples filing jointly, you can have a combined AGI of $150,000 to $160,000. The contribution limit is reduced at the $150,000 level, and is completely eliminated when it reaches $160,000. While you can't deduct a Roth IRA contribution from your annual taxes, it grows tax-free. So, when you retire and withdraw your Roth IRA, you'll owe no taxes on it.

Let's return to our previous example to see how it works tax-free. Imagine that you've contributed $4,000 per year for forty-four years at a 10 percent return. Your deposits total $176,000, but compounding works its magic. At the time of withdrawal you have $2,871,619—tax-free! If, instead of the Roth, you put $4,000 each year into a taxable savings account and you were in the 31 percent tax bracket, your account would be worth $1,105,399; a difference of $1,766,220. Right there is the answer to the common question, "What difference would a $4,000-a-year Roth really make? It's just $4,000, after all."

One of my best bits of advice to younger clients is to take advantage of the Roth IRA: "Use it or lose it," I warn them. Often I talk to people starting out in their careers. Though everything seems like small potatoes when you're just starting out, it's easy to do a lot of good then. Compounding is really on their side. Over time, their income is bound to rise. And I know that it's more comfortable setting funds aside when you have more discretionary income—the early years are often lean times. But before these people know it, they'll be too successful to qualify for a Roth. Most of them don't know what this opportunity represents, and I'd hate to see them miss out. I explain that my affluent clients would love to have an extra investment vehicle that's permanently tax-free. *Carpe diem!*

Tax Deferral

When I talk to clients and suggest deferring their taxes, many say, "Why bother? I'm going to end up paying them anyway." They hear the word *deferral* and think "inevitable and equal." Yes, you pay taxes on certain investment yields, but you can minimize that exposure, keeping more of what you make. In short, your tax load comes out to "inevitable, but less."

So my rule of thumb is invest now, rather than paying that tax. It'll mean a smaller tax bite, overall. Nowadays, the tax code is set up to help you defer paying, and for as long as possible. The government has confidence in you!

Remember your mom's hypothetical success in the market? She started with a $1,000 nest egg, investing another $1,000 a year to her retirement account. She stayed with it for forty-four years and saved up $717,905 while deferring taxes.

Yes, sooner or later, 31 percent would come due in taxes. But consider the numbers. If Mom paid taxes in year 44 as a lump sum, she'd be left with $495,354. However, most of us take some out each year when we retire, deferring the taxes until the next year. By contrast, if she'd paid annually, she'd have short-circuited her tax-deferred compounding. At the end of year 44, Mom would have kept only $276,249. So even after she paid her taxes she kept more of her money.

A number of other retirement vehicles, like the 401(k), also let you deduct and defer taxes. If you're self-employed, you can open a SEP IRA. The limits are even higher than a 401(k)'s. Rather than $14,000, your cap is $40,000 per year, or 25 percent of your gross income—whichever is less. Alternatively, you could start a profit-sharing plan (PSP). Again, you put in the lesser of two amounts: up to 15 percent of your gross, or $25,500 per year. Obviously, a PSP is less of a commitment, which helps if you're a new enterprise or want flexibility for some other reason. You're not locked into a set percentage. In very lean times, you can even drop your contribution to 0 percent.

Inflation

In terms of your prosperity, inflation poses an even greater risk than taxes. All the tax-free investments in the world aren't enough if you can't keep pace with inflation. And that's a real issue. Our average life expectancy is now 84.6 years for women and 81.6 years for men.

Like Midas's alchemy, that prospect is a mixed blessing. Yes, most Americans can now look forward to a long life. With luck, you'll always have loved ones around you, and you won't turn any of them into gold. But whether your later years will be financially as well as emotionally rich is up to you. Maintaining your income stream can be tricky—unless you plan, in which case your reward is the best of both worlds.

We must all brace for the fact that, over time, everything costs more. You may be surprised to learn what things cost twenty years ago in 1984. A gallon of gas was seventy-five cents and a movie ticket cost $3.00. The car you could purchase then for $21,000 would cost you $44,000 today. Twenty years ago Medicare paid $800 for a night in the hospital. Today it's $1,647!

If you're a parent, the plot thickens. A college education has risen 6 percent per year in the past ten years alone. Then consider that today's average full-time student spends $1,750 a year on pizza and beer. I'm serious! Thirty years ago that was a year's tuition.

Sundry tidbits like these boil down to one simple equation: When prices rise just 3 percent per year, they'll have doubled in twenty-four years. And not only do things cost more; your purchasing power sinks. Yes, all that's manageable if your salary keeps pace. But here's how your investments can do even more for you, exponentially bringing wealth as time passes. Remember our goal is not to get by; it's to prosper.

Let's start with one key assumption. Your investments' rate of return must exceed inflation plus taxes. It's not just feasible; it's vital. And it's why parking your money in a 3 percent-yield savings account is a losing proposition. Listen now, while you can still change your future in a big way. Your one purpose for a savings account is to stockpile three to six months' worth of emergency living expenses. That's it. Once you've built that reserve, it's time to invest.

Diversification

Let's revert to our workout metaphor and the fine art of cross-training, which is the final element of your capacity-building drills. Picture all the cardiovascular classes out there. Which programs does your fitness center or club offer? Then think back over the years. Along the way, maybe you tried aerobics (what outfits!), and you may even have longed to be Jamie Lee Curtis or John Travolta in *Perfect*. Perhaps you took a step class, spin class, or power boxing. There were plenty of others, too.

As a newcomer to fitness, you probably were looking for that "silver bullet" to melt pounds and build muscle. Hey, why not? Certain programs are proven to work better than others. But each has its limitations. Many of us view investing in similar terms: What's the answer? Is it large-cap growth, technology, real estate, or fixed-income plans? We're constantly seeking the next hot stock or investment. To tell the truth, though, there's no magic formula for snagging the right investment. Your best course of action is diversification, also known as asset allocation. Both terms mean the same thing: As that long-forgotten French peasant put it, "Don't put all your eggs in one basket." See the Morningstar® style boxes at Morningstar.com for more help getting started.

Let's talk about a very important study, "The Determinants of Portfolio Performance," by Gary Brinson, Randolph Hood, and Gilbert Beebower.[2] This study won the Nobel Prize in Economics and is as "real world" as we get. The key finding was that 90 percent of your returns come from how well your assets are diversified. That's right: Only 10 percent of your return comes from market timing and stock selection. In other words, if you averaged 10 percent in your portfolio for the last eight years, most of each year's return came from how you allocated your funds; just a tenth resulted from timing and specific stock picks. A pittance, right?

Yet many people think that being a successful investor is simply a matter of market timing and stock selection. Americans have a widespread misconception that all it takes is the ability (or luck) to grab winners and ditch stinkers. Yet for most of us, this strategy doesn't deliver consistent returns. Instead, the hot-fingers approach often generates needless stress and anxiety.

After years of meeting with people face-to-face, I've grown convinced that emotions are the central factor in the whole investment equation. You and my clients, though, have a primo alternative to fretting: asset allocation.

Done right, it's a process. You build a diversified portfolio by mixing the three basic asset classes: cash, bonds, and stocks. Your risk-tolerance determines the ratios. How much do you value prospects of gain versus security?

Before assessing your risk tolerance, we'll need to take an inventory of your portfolio. It's critical to compare dollars across all categories. That frees you from "mental accounting," a whiz economist's term for the unconscious habit of segregating dollars by source, location, or use. People tend to divide their money into "mental" accounts, each with a different importance. As a result, we value some dollars less than others and waste or underutilize them.

You know what I mean; we all do it. By rights, $100 from your salary, tax refund, or roulette winnings should hold the same significance. But we're not always the most rational beings. By attaching labels, we give ourselves permission to treat these "various" dollars differently. We think nothing of using those roulette winnings to buy a round of drinks for our friends. So I encourage you to break down the mental walls that divide your holdings.

Let's look at an example. Imagine that you keep $75,000 in a fixed annuity and $200,000 in various stock funds in your 401(k). Back in the glow of 1999, many of my new clients were thrilled to get 20 percent growth from a 401(k), but they were dejected by an annuity's lowly 5 percent. But in 2001, when everyone's stocks took a pounding, an annuity's 6 percent return had them pumped. I can't tell you how many clients came to me then, saying things like, "Standing at that party, I felt so proud to tell my brother-in-law my annuity's return!" Still, the same people would often continue by telling me, "But I really regret not selling the stock funds earlier, when I should have."

Rather than worrying about picking plum stocks, just diversify. All too often, I speak to employees who have 40 percent and more of their investment in their company stock. They're hardly alone. A study called "Mental Accounting Matters," conducted by Richard Thaler of the University of Chicago, found that employees offered company stock considered investments in their firms to be distinct from other equity choices.[3] They typically held 42 percent in their company stock, with the balance split evenly between fixed-income and equity funds. If company stock wasn't an option, the typical allocation was 50 percent in stocks and 50 percent in bonds. I always advise clients to hold no more than 10 percent of any company in their portfolio. I've seen some very nasty falls, like the ones former employees of Lucent Technologies and WorldCom took, that could have been prevented had the client come to me first.

When you create your own asset allocation, you also need to be aware of a few pitfalls. First is "naive diversification." It means letting the investment choices presented dictate your asset allocation. According to another study, if people were offered more equity funds, they tended to allocate more to equities. If offered more fixed-income choices, then more of their money would go to fixed income. This can be a problem because you should weight your choices according to your personal goals, not what the company is offering you. It depends on personal factors: your age, time horizon, risk tolerance, income, and a number of other variables. Eventually it all comes down to asset allocation.

Of course, everyone has different goals, time horizons, and risk tolerances. So your portfolio needs to reflect *your* priorities and nobody else's. Granted, sometimes you'll have to hang tough while someone crows that you should've taken their advice. It's worth it. If you're into rowing, don't let someone drag you to the mall every weekend when you could be out sculling.

You and I agree that a "workout plan" will serve you well. But remember, it only works if you do it. To follow through, you must derive some pleasure or satisfaction in the process. What kinds of workouts do you enjoy? Maybe you like running on an outdoor track, or you swim laps every other lunchtime with a friend from work. Or you walk fast enough through a mall to get your heart rate up.

For some, a rough-and-ready game of hoops in a neighbor's driveway is the ultimate. There are dozens of routes to cardiovascular wellness. Go it alone or in front of a cheering throng; either way, you'll do a lot for your body if you're choosing the method you most enjoy.

You also have to make sure your investments suit your needs as well. For instance, it wouldn't make sense for someone who wants to buy a home in three years to sink everything into risky small-cap stocks. Nor should people who hope to retire in fifteen years tie up their retirement accounts in CDs or savings accounts. The key is to create a portfolio that minimizes risk while maximizing potential returns—again, to the degree that makes sense for you.

There are a number of ways to reduce your risk. Too often I see investors chase returns by buying whatever did well the previous year. That's not a waste, yet there are better ways to go.

Now let's look at all diversification's potential benefits. Imagine that back in 1984, you decided to be a contrarian. No herd mentality for you! You committed $10,000 a year to whichever asset class performed worst the year before. Each January you held to that strategy and added a new $10,000. By the end of 2003, your $200,000 base investment would have grown to $493,723. Not brilliant, perhaps, but better than many.

The thing is, most people I know aren't contrarians. And, I've noticed, they prefer investing their "fresh" $10,000 in the prior year's top asset class. There are worse ways to go, sure. If you'd done that in our scenario, you'd have accumulated $596,775 by our last New Year's Eve—20 percent more than a contrarian.

But what if every year you'd said, "I don't know which category will have the best performance, so I'll spread it equally among all of them."

Canny you! Your $200,000 base investment would have mushroomed to $695,074.

Now, I can understand your supposing that's as good as it gets, but let's go it one better. More often than not, a new star is rising or the old one's luster has diminished. So I recommend you adopt this easy strategy. First, take your new $10,000 and spread it equally among the major asset classes (equity growth funds, bond funds, international, etc.). Then rebalance your portfolio each year so that throughout the twenty years, your funds remain divided equally between all the asset classes. In our model, by the end of 2003, you'd have saved a dizzying $729,884. It's simply banking on the cyclical nature of investments. For more on asset classes, see the Callan Periodic Table in Appendix B.

What's Your Asset Allocation?

In terms of mixing cash, bonds, and stocks, where do you think you'll spend most of your time, knowing what you've learned? Not in picking stocks, but rather in choosing how to diversify. From the Investment Inventory you completed previously, you know what your current investable assets are. Now, let's learn *which* types of investments you hold in those accounts.

Take out your statements, and I'll show you how to figure out the asset classes. They generally fall into the following categories of stocks or bonds:

Stocks

Large-Cap Value	Large-Cap Growth	Large-Cap Blend
Mid-Cap Value	Mid-Cap Growth	Mid-Cap Blend
Small-Cap Value	Small-Cap Growth	Small-Cap Blend
Foreign		

Bonds

Maturity

Short-Term	Intermediate-Term	Long-Term

High-Yield

Corporate	International	Government

This exercise builds an overview of how your assets are held. Granted, it may take a bit of sleuthing. Many of you will be focusing primarily on your 401(k)s, IRAs, Roth IRAs, other retirement plans, and children's education accounts, simply because that's where most of your investable assets are at the moment.

There are two ways to find out which asset classes your investments belong to. First, you can look up a mutual fund's ticker symbol at Morningstar.com. It will tell you the various asset classes of your fund. Or go by the fund's title. If it says International in the title, you can probably guess it's a foreign fund. If the fund is called Growth and Income or Equity Income, it's probably a value fund. The purpose of this exercise is to make sure you don't own two, three, or more funds that you think are "diversified" and really all come under the same asset class.

Imagine that you coach a basketball team. The team has twenty players. How do you decide who plays? Maybe you look at those players who have done best in the past year and rely chiefly on them. But you also cycle in your average performers, knowing that they could turn into strong players. Be sure to keep playing all those asset classes!

■ ■ ■

How do you feel about the results from the various investing exercises you just worked through? Does it seem like a lot of work? Don't let that deter you. As I've said, a few changes can make all the difference. And I'll be the first to admit that, like cardiovascular work, investments are sometimes tough going.

Successful investing takes a strong focus, a measure of persistence, and routine monitoring. Sometimes you'll get an endorphin high—"Honey, check out these returns!" But more often, you'll just chug along. The key is to remember your fundamentals.

Certain things will keep you motivated and optimize your workout's benefits, such as wanting to retire at 60 or pay for your daughter's wedding. Would you want to run a marathon alone? Or bypass the finish line with one mile left? Where's the satisfaction in that? Besides, how could you measure your performance? To improve, you must figure out what needs adjusting and where you want to be. In the same way, be an active participant in your investment planning. Take charge today!

A Final Note About Women and Investing

Investing is crucial for everyone, but gender gives men an edge in terms of retirement holdings. The longer life expectancy that's usually thought of as a woman's advantage also strains her finances.

The facts for women get harsh, but I feel it's my duty to inform women out there—and the men on whom they may rely. While 80 percent of men die married, 80 percent of women die single. Most widows now living in poverty weren't poor when their husbands were alive.

Let's start with the good news and problem-solve from there. Today's American woman has more chances for financial security than any ancestress from any nation. Management and professional positions, including entrepreneurial roles, are far more common. Companies owned by women are growing at twice the rate of all small businesses in the nation. More than 30 percent of women today earn more than their husbands. In sum, women earn more, have higher future earnings, possess more discretionary income, and control more equity and capital. As a rule, these women will reach age 65 with more savings and retirement benefits. It's the proverbial no-brainer.

Women have other advantages. We tend to be more careful shoppers when it comes to investments. We ask a lot of questions. And women also don't trade nearly as often as men, which gives us an edge. Maybe you or your beloved wants to take a class on investing. If so, I say "Brava!" but I strongly recommend a class that focuses on asset allocation rather than timing the market.

Here I should note the three big reasons women have their work cut out for them with investing. First, they live longer than men and tend to be younger than their husbands. Second, the majority of women earn less: Even employed full-time, their 2002 median earnings were $29,680, or 31 percent less than the men's median of $38,884. Even education doesn't close the gender gap. In 2000, college-educated women earned just $5,000 more than male high-school graduates.[4] Third, the typical woman puts in far fewer hours in the workforce. She typically works thirty-two years, compared with the typical man's forty-four years. Plus, a larger proportion of a woman's years in the workplace are spent in part-time work. At some point, the lady of the house usually trims her work hours to care for a child or parent.

That earnings shortfall is exacerbated by the fact that only 10 percent of working women retire with pensions. In 1996, Social Security paid an average of $621 per month to retired females. And let's not forget that a woman today is less likely to marry. More and more women are remaining single; we now comprise over 25 percent of America's adults. Being self-sufficient can be a plus, but the lifestyle brings certain habits that cost extra. This group tends to spend more money on what the Department of Agriculture calls "food prepared away from home," as well as on cars, entertainment, beauty treatments, and other nonessentials.

Then there's the divorce question. When couples divide their assets, equal doesn't always mean equitable. A true fifty-fifty split takes an awareness of certain facts. The statistics are compelling: Divorce's financial impact is usually far greater for women than for men. Immediately following a divorce, women age 50 and older experience a 39 percent decline in income, which is nearly triple that of men's at 14 percent. One year after a divorce, 40 percent of men have regained their predivorce incomes, while only 21 percent of women have.

Even when part-time-employee women start spending more time in the workplace, their earnings are likely to be less than those of career women. We hear a lot about B-school alumnae leaving their corner suites to host playgroups, but all this press coverage distorts reality. Most divorced women's earnings are far more modest.

When I sit down with recently divorced female clients, I find many of them had no idea they had to stay married ten years to qualify for a share of their husband's Social Security benefits—current or eventual.

Women also change jobs more often than men, holding a given job an average of 4.8 years. Consequently, we often miss out on pensions and company-match retirement vesting, which typically happens at the five-year mark.

At work, I do my absolute best to protect people against tragic mistakes. Even with newly married clients, I discuss the financial implications of the chief breadwinner's demise. This information is especially vital if the breadwinner's pension is supposed to be the couple's primary source of retirement income—no matter how many years away that is. Often, Mr. or Mrs. Breadwinner chooses a lifetime payout from the pension's annuity. Once that decision is made and retirement has occurred, everything's set in stone and there needs to be a backup plan for the unthinkable.

It's one thing if the household's chief breadwinner lives longest, since he's already set to receive a monthly check for his entire life anyway. But if the breadwinner dies first, the check goes with him (or her) and that income self-destructs.

I strongly recommend a technique called Pension Maximization (or Pension Max, for short). It entails buying a life-insurance policy on the chief breadwinner. The coverage should equal any income you'd lose once his annuity was compromised. It's hard enough for a family to lose a spouse, especially by surprise, without losing their lifestyle, too.

Maybe your spouse hasn't hit retirement age yet. You still have choices. On retirement, you have the option of taking a lump-sum distribution. That's often the preferable way to go. You can transfer the lump-sum distribution into an IRA rollover and continue to defer taxes until you withdraw from it. You need to understand all your options and the tax implications of your decisions.

Married life parallels certain patterns of singlehood. In either case, women tend to make different investment choices from men. Like less-educated or lower-income Americans, they tend to be fiscally conservative. Two major studies confirm this tendency. For instance, women in the federal Thrift Savings Plan allocated a smaller share of their investments to equities than men did. So often I hear women say, "Look, this is all I have. If something goes wrong, I'm sunk." I understand their predicament, especially in view of the income patterns that recur among couples.

Couples tend to adopt one investment style, with certain patterns. For instance, a woman whose husband owns stocks and bonds tends to focus on bonds, bypassing stocks—which she thinks of as iffy. Yet influence can flow the other way, too. Men married to women who own bonds buy more bonds than other men do. Another intriguing wrinkle: If a household owns an IRA as well as a 401(k), both husband and wife are more apt to invest in stocks. It seems that, having made retirement planning a priority, such couples came to know and appreciate the stock market. Besides, on average, they have more assets to work with. It's like athletes who are exposed to the best new methods and tools: They're more apt to use them, combine them, and benefit from venturing into areas where they're not proficient.

NOTES

1. Gary Belsky and Thomas Gilovich, *Why Smart People Make Big Money Mistakes.* (New York: Simon and Schuster, 1999).

2. Gary Brinson, Randolph Hood, and Gilbert Beebower. "The Determinants of Portfolio Performance," *Financial Analyst Journal*, v. 42, no. 4, (July-August 1986), pp. 39–48.

3. Richard H. Thaler, "Mental Accounting Matters," *Journal of Behavioral Decision Making*, v. 12, 1999, pp. 183–206.

4. Kate Lorenz, "Pay: The Gender Gap," Careerbuilder .com (accessed April 24, 2004).

GETTING IT ALL TOGETHER

OVER THE LAST SEVEN CHAPTERS, I've asked you to work hard and challenge yourself. I've guided you through a workout and taught you a process that will keep your finances healthy for the rest of your life. You know how you feel stretched and invigorated after finishing an ambitious and energetic workout? How your self-esteem has increased because you realize how much you're capable of achieving? That's how I hope you feel now about your finances!

Throughout this book you've learned that doing a few smart things to enhance your financial fitness can literally create thousands of dollars of net worth for yourself—even with your present income. By now, I'm sure that you understand that financial fitness, like physical fitness, is a matter of doing the most with what you have. You might not have been blessed with the world's greatest physique or have the genes of an Olympian, but we all know your body can accomplish much more when it's fit. Similarly, regardless of how high or low your income may be, your money will work harder for you when it's managed well.

I was recently reminiscing with my client Catherine about how much progress she has made over the last few years. Four years ago, she had $24,000 put away for her retirement; today she has over $125,000! She didn't sell her home and move to a cheaper neighborhood; she didn't sell her car and buy a clunker; and she didn't restrict herself to eating nothing but macaroni and cheese for dinner. She simply did the workout faithfully and reaped the rewards over just a few years.

I was so proud of her when she told me she was now saving 15 percent of her income! Her new goal is to get to 20 percent. She's also paid off all her credit card debts and is working toward having $12,000 in a savings account "just in case." She feels terrific about how she's handling her money, and I'm thrilled to have been a part of the transformation. These are the kinds of results you can enjoy in the future just by making the Net Worth Workout a way of life.

POWER IN SYNERGY

By now you're accustomed to doing the Net Worth Workout for each of your financial quadrants. But the final step in the workout—and the most important one—is to bring all the elements of your financial life together and get them working in harmony with each other over the long term. There's power in synergy. With the Net Worth Workout, as with a great fitness plan, the whole is greater than the sum of the individual parts, and the greatest benefits come when all the elements work together to support each other.

For example, if you're trying to lose weight and firm your physique, you probably know that you'll get the best results by combining a nutrition-packed, protein-rich diet plan with an aerobic workout and strength training. If you did just one of these things, you'd probably still see some benefits. But if you were to incorporate all of them in a cohesive workout plan, you'll get much more dramatic results, because your efforts in one area would enhance your efforts in the others. Weight lifting builds muscle, and muscle building burns fat. The protein-rich diet fuels the muscle-building process, and the aerobic workout boosts your metabolism, so the fat-burning and muscle-building processes work more efficiently.

In the same way, when you harmonize your income-earning efforts with your spending plan, saving schedule, and investment strategy, each quadrant will boost the efficiency of the others. For example, a slight rise in your earnings can boost saving for a home, which in turn allows you to make a larger down payment and have lower monthly mortgage payments (spending). Similarly, spending less on lunch can give you more to add to your 401(k) account (investing), which will reduce your taxes today and increase how much money you'll have when you retire. And saving prudently can help keep your spending plan on track if you should run into some unexpected expenses. As you well know by now, when you maximize the synergy among the four quadrants (see Figure 8-1), you maximize your potential to achieve financial fitness.

By now, you've seen that even small efforts, like saving an extra one percent or 2 percent more from each paycheck, can have quite an impact on your life and certainly can reduce stress and worry and ease tensions. The truth is that we only get a few opportunities to make really massive strides in our financial lives, but we have abundant opportunities every day to make small, incremental changes. You might have a chance to save $1,000 on a new car once in a

FIGURE 8-1. FINANCIAL HEALTH QUADRANTS—REVISITED.

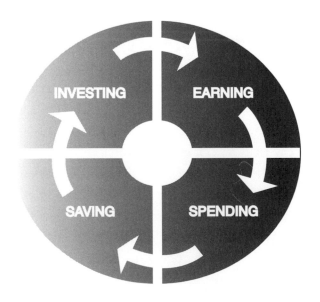

while, but you have at least a thousand opportunities to save a dollar in the course of a single year. Or look at it this way: The opportunities to negotiate the price of your home by $10,000 or hammer out the terms of a salary raise are infrequent. But small changes in the way you contribute to or invest in your 401(k) or IRA can create tens of thousands of dollars for you over your lifetime. For the most part, net worth is built not of giant, earth-shaking efforts, but of many small efforts focused on a common goal. It's all about creating and maintaining a healthy financial lifestyle. Because of that, coordinating your efforts in all four financial quadrants is essential. It will allow you to maximize earning, control spending, increase savings, and optimize investments. And that means you'll be able to enjoy more peace today and live more comfortably in the future.

PREPARE . . . THEN JUST DO IT

So how do you coordinate the four financial quadrants so they work together?

You do it, essentially, by "just doing it," as Nike says. The more you do it, the more it becomes a part of your everyday life and the more proficient you become at it. Of course, you'll make a few slips along the way, but nothing that will throw you off track. And when you've reached the point where you've achieved the "flow" I talked about in Chapter Two, that's when you'll realize the greatest benefits from using the workout. But, just as you wouldn't go for a run without first deciding what route to take and checking the weather, you need to make sure you don't omit any steps of this financial workout. You definitely want to know where you're going and what type of conditions you may face.

As you'll remember, "flow" is what happens when your concentration is so strong that you're totally absorbed in whatever activity you're involved in. It's the state of mind that athletes strive for—feeling totally alert, completely in control, and at the peak of their abilities. But for professional athletes, getting to that point is a process, a skill acquired over time. And virtually every flow-producing activity requires you to do some hard work before it becomes enjoyable. When you start your workout, the first quarter-hour or so might seem like a bit of a struggle. Our bodies resist what we're asking them to do. But once we adjust, we start feeling much better.

Achieving that flow in your finances isn't any different. Simply because you're not accustomed to doing it, financial planning is hard at first. But once you've warmed up, once you get into the flow, you begin to feel exactly the same way an athlete does when she's achieved that state. In fact, like athletes, people who create wealth go through this cycle over and over again. Millionaires take some time every week to *plan* their investments—it's part of their practice. It means sitting down and thinking about what kind of investments are going to provide them with the greatest return, or meeting with their financial adviser regularly to analyze their performance. Like the first quarter-hour of a workout, planning isn't necessarily a lot of fun, but these millionaires work through the uncomfortable part because they're going for the flow. And in the meantime, they're building up emotional strength and resilience.

It doesn't have to be drudgery. You can do a few things to make this process more enjoyable. Perhaps you'll reward yourself once you're finished. I like to light scented candles because it creates a very soothing atmosphere when I'm doing the Net Worth Workout. You may want to put on some good music while you're doing it. Gyms always have televisions in their workout areas and many people have iPods or headphones to get into the groove of their physical workout. Experiment to discover the best environment, where you'll be as productive as possible. I sincerely hope you enjoy this time. The payoff will come from your feeling more in control of your finances and having more time with your family and friends.

PUTTING IT TOGETHER: THE LIFESTYLE LOG

Using your Lifestyle Log, which you read about in Chapter Five, is a good way to get warmed up and an excellent—and easy—way to start coordinating the quadrants. Although it will take some time and effort the first time you put together the log, once you get used to doing it you'll find that it doesn't take more than about an hour a month to maintain. What I'd suggest you do, then, is every month, after you've filled out the log, look back over it to see what your strong points are and what your Achilles' heel is.

The first time you put together your Lifestyle Log you

discovered what you need each month to maintain your lifestyle. Perhaps you learned that you too (like 50 percent of Americans) have succumbed to the Spending Rule of Thumb, spending as much money as you earn. As difficult as this may be to discover, congratulate yourself for having the courage to confront the situation!

I've mentioned that the average American works forty-four years, then retires with a $44,000 net worth. That represents just $1,000 for every year worked! Meanwhile, if the average American had only invested that $1,000 annually in the S&P 500 for forty-four years, at age 65, she would have $717,905! Ask yourself, "What happened to that $673,000 of "missing" net worth? That's why it's critical for you to get the most out of each and every financial health quadrant. What's your missing net worth? Is it $10,000, $100,000, even $1 million? Dream big, and hopefully you can see how small changes in each quadrant can make big differences in your net worth!

USING YOUR NET WORTH STATEMENT TO COORDINATE THE QUADRANTS

Another good way to get accustomed to coordinating the quadrants is to go over your Net Worth Statement (see Chapter Three) every three months. Public companies release quarterly reports to let their stockholders know how they're doing. Think of this as a quarterly report on your own favorite enterprise—you! Like using the Lifestyle Log, going over the statement can help you coordinate the quadrants by seeing which assets are helping you accelerate your net worth and which liabilities are the most hindrance to growing your net worth. Here's an example of how it works:

My client Alistair loves cars and has two of them—a four-wheel-drive truck he takes to the mountains for skiing and a sporty convertible he uses to head out to the beach on summer weekends. One quarter, when he was reviewing his Net Worth Statement, he noticed that he had listed the cars as being worth $10,000 and $8,000, respectively. He takes good care of his vehicles, so they're both running fine, even though they have plenty of mileage on them. Even so, when he thought about how much they were worth, he realized it didn't make sense to pay as much as he was for auto insurance. So he contacted his insurance company and had them raise the deductible from $250 to $1,000. That cut his insurance bill by 15 percent, which he then took and put into a fund he had set up to save for the house he was planning to buy.

Here's another example. Until Jane put her Net Worth Statement together, she never realized that the $10,000 she put in a savings account was only earning 3 percent, or $300 a year, which she now knows means a return of $225 after taxes. Meanwhile, because of her $8,000 balance on her credit card, *she paid* over $1,480 each year in interest payments. Seeing the difference in black and white motivated her to switch her credit card to one with zero percent financing and pay the debt off as quickly as possible. She then used that $1,480 "savings" (or $123 each month) to start a college-savings 529 plan for her son, Jack. Even better, she now adds that $123 every month to this fund and has shopped around for a savings account that pays 4 percent for her $10,000.

Another good way to get all the quadrants coordinated and working for you is to use a strengths and weaknesses exercise on a quarterly basis, in conjunction with the Net Worth Statement. So, every three months, after you've made a Net Worth Statement, go back and check out your previous statement. Based on that comparison, make a list of what you consider to be your current strengths and weaknesses in each quadrant. This exercise should help you identify your trouble spots. Of course, you can write down as many strengths/weaknesses as you want for each quadrant. Just to give you an idea, though, Figure 8-2 gives examples of one strength and one weakness for each financial health quadrant. Once you have spotted your weaknesses, also write in next to them what you are going to do to change them and write a specific date by which you will have accomplished your goal.

For example, at fifty years old, Anthony had accumulated a sizable amount for his retirement. He was planning on getting married for the first time and wanted to be sure he and his fiancée could retire comfortably at age 65 and travel the world! He did the Net Worth Statement and discovered that he was only contributing 6 percent of his income to his 401(k). He increased it to the maximum contribution and took advantage of the catch-up provision for people over age 50. This allowed him to contribute the usual $15,000 to his plan and then an additional $5,000

FIGURE 8-2. SAMPLE STRENGTHS AND WEAKNESSES EXERCISE.

Strengths

Earning:	Increased my income by 10 percent.
Spending:	Reduced spending on clothes by 20 percent.
Saving:	Saved 15 percent of my gross income.
Investing:	Researched my 401(k) choices and selected funds that outperformed their peers.

Weaknesses

Earning:	Didn't participate in transportation spending account, which would have saved $250 in the last quarter. Sign up for this program by next week.
Spending:	Overspent by $500 on things for the home this month. Will reduce that spending for the next three months.
Saving:	Haven't saved six months of living expenses for emergencies. Open a savings account and have $200 a month automatically credited to it from my checking account by next week.
Investing:	Haven't rebalanced my portfolio since last year. Set up appointment in the next two weeks with my financial adviser to review this portfolio.

on top of that. By making this change, he saw that if he wanted to stop working earlier he could, because this extra saving would help him generate more income ten years from now. Best of all, he didn't miss the money that was being redirected to the 401(k) because most of it was being eaten up by taxes.

In doing these warm-up exercises, though, it's important

you remember that they are just warm-ups. That is, they're just intended to get you started on thinking about your finances on a regular basis. If you start spending an hour or two every month, you can just as quickly build up to one hour every week and eventually two hours every week. Remember, that second hour is crucial. Thinking about your finances for over eight hours a month brings you to a learning threshold and lets you internalize certain key principles. So "just do it," because that's what the millionaires are doing!

NOBODY'S PERFECT

Realistically, you should understand that all the quadrants won't be working perfectly and seamlessly 100 percent of the time. Although I encourage you to strive for optimal performance, I don't want you to expect perfect results from your efforts. That's a sure way to end up on the wrong track. If you'll accept nothing less than perfection, I guarantee you'll get so bogged down in frustration that your motivation and resolve will fizzle away.

A client of mine by the name of Kirsten learned this lesson the hard way. After her income had increased because of a big promotion, she found herself splurging on things she normally could not afford. At first she enjoyed it, but when she tried to stop—and couldn't—she got so angry with herself that she fell into the defeatist attitude that derails so many would-be dieters: "I can't do it! I just don't have the self-discipline!" She was literally about to give up on her savings plan because of this one setback. I advised her not to be too hard on herself because it was all those years of "sweat equity" that got her to this point where she had earned the promotion. She had a right to enjoy her success—within reason. As long as she kept things in check and reined herself in after her "celebratory spending," she'd be fine.

Another potential pitfall is a serious downturn in the investing quadrant. Many of us have seen the value of our 401(k)s cut in half, and that feels pretty lousy. As a result of this downturn, a lot of people abandoned their savings efforts because watching their retirement accounts dwindle was too discouraging. Some people have even stopped contributing to their 401(k)s—which is a huge mistake. They are turning a significant loss into an even greater loss, because for every dollar they fail to put into their fund, they also miss out on a matching dollar from their employers. When your employer matches your contribution you are guaranteeing yourself a 50 percent return! You put $100 into your 401(k) and your employer adds $50 on your behalf, so your $100 investment automatically becomes $150; that's the 50 percent return! You need that 50 percent match more than ever when times get tough.

HOW THE NET WORTH WORKOUT HELPS IN TOUGH TIMES

Don't fall into the trap of getting discouraged and giving up on your workout. One of the Net Worth Workout's greatest advantages is that it can be of enormous help when times are tough. When one quadrant is weak, you can use your strengths in the other quadrants to shore it up. Sometimes, a temporary setback in one quadrant can be a blessing in disguise. In fact, if you quit saving and investing when things look bleak, you'll miss out on some of the best opportunities to strengthen your net worth—like buying stocks when their prices are cheaper. When other investors are wringing their hands, the smartest investors are ringing their brokers. When there's a downturn in the market, you can take an additional chunk of your savings to buy more of your favorite stock or mutual fund.

But the best possible way to respond to tough times is to harness the power of all four quadrants to help pull you through. Last fall my client Teresa lost her job. She came to me during the first week of her unemployment to work out a plan for weathering this unexpected storm. Even though she had three or four months of income squirreled away, she was thinking of doing occasional substitute teaching or working in a bookstore part-time to keep money coming in, while still leaving business hours free to tackle job interviews. I told her this was a smart policy because she could then stretch her three-month emergency fund to six or eight months if she had to. After all, she had no way of knowing how long it might take to land a decent new job.

When I asked her what she'd do if her job hunt stretched to eight or nine months, she looked at me with fear in her eyes. I grabbed a piece of paper and we quickly worked out a way to temporarily trim $400 from her monthly budget. Until she found her new job, she'd wash clothes at home instead of taking them to the corner laundry service, mow the grass herself instead of paying a landscaping company, and read or watch TV at night instead of going to the movies or out to dinner. She'd also have to put her savings plan on hold for the duration of her unemployment, but we agreed to meet again when she landed her new job to work out a plan to make up for what she'd lost. She also realized she could cash in a few short-term bonds from her portfolio and use the dividends from some stocks to supplement her reduced income.

Teresa called me about five months later to announce the start of her great new job. Her finances had gotten slightly out of shape, but she'd recover within six months because she had coordinated her quadrants to pull her through. Although she had temporarily used her savings to replace her income, she kept up by adding at least some new income so that her savings didn't take the full hit. She'd tapped into her investments to supplement her expenses with passive income. And she had temporarily reduced her spending to limit the strain on the other three quadrants. Best of all, she actually had two job offers, and with the knowledge she'd gained from the Net Worth Workout she was able to carefully consider the benefits packages of each and choose the job with the better plan. Now she had a new job that she loved, and as her income-earning ability recovered its full strength, she worked to restore all four quadrants to their previous good health.

HOW THE NET WORTH WORKOUT HELPS YOU PREPARE FOR RETIREMENT

As you do the Net Worth Workout throughout your working years, remember that your ultimate long-term goal is to replace your active income with passive income. That is, to create enough net worth to provide for your needs throughout your retirement. The Net Worth Workout enables you to do that by developing your financial health in all areas—your income (i.e., earnings), spending, saving, and investing.

However, despite all the help the workout provides you in preparing for retirement, the one question it can't answer for you is how much money you really need to amass in order to live the way you'd like to when you stop working. That is, how much is enough? Some people try to guesstimate this figure. They say, "Well, if I have $2 million by the time I'm sixty-five, that should be enough." But would it be? By today's standards, $2 million is a very big number. But how much of that money is really yours to spend? It depends on whether it's calculated before or after taxes. If you have $2 million in an IRA, by the time you've finished paying the taxes on it, all you'll have left is about $1.3 million. That's still a good amount of money, but would it be enough?

Of course, if you're contributing to a Roth IRA, since you're investing after taxes, when you retire and begin to withdraw money from your retirement account you'll be able to do it tax-free. On the other hand, if you contribute to your retirement account before taxes, you have to pay the taxes when you withdraw money from the account. That is, if you withdraw $5,000 each month, for example, Uncle Sam will ask for his share, just as he did when you earned $5,000 a month from your job. Fortunately, only your withdrawals are taxable—whatever remains in the IRA continues to grow tax-deferred. But the bottom line is that if you haven't figured Uncle Sam's slice of your retirement pie, now is the time to start calculating your retirement income with two numbers instead of one—both before and after taxes.

Unfortunately, taxation isn't the only thing endangering your retirement funds. You've got an even greater menace to contend with, and one that's much more insidious. Let's say you're forty-one years old now and you plan to start using that $2 million (or $1.3 million after taxes) when you're sixty-five—which is twenty-four years from now. I know what you're thinking: $1.3 million seems like plenty to retire on. And it would be . . . if you were retiring *today*. But there's a problem: $1.3 million of today's dollars will only be worth about $650,000 twenty-four years from now. You'll have the same number of dollars, but their actual buying power will have been cut virtually in half because of inflation.

Unfortunately, there's no way to stop inflation, but there is a way to plan for it. You can begin by mastering "the Rule of 72." According to the Rule of 72, if you want to find the number of years it will take to double your money at a certain inflation rate you divide the inflation rate into seventy-two. (You can also use the rule for interest rates.) That means that at a 3 percent inflation rate, what is worth $2 million today will cost $4 million in twenty-four years (72 / 3 = 24). If inflation is 4 percent, then in eighteen years your money would need to double. Of course, not everything you buy is going to go up by 3 percent a year—that's just an average. But one way or the other, inflation is going to take a big bite out of your retirement funds, so it's essential that you take that into account when figuring out how much money you'll need after you stop working.

How Much Do I Really Need to Retire?

If you're like most people, you probably think that you'll be able to scale back your lifestyle once you retire. "I won't need the $3,000 a month I'm living on now," you might be telling yourself. "I'll be able to make do just fine on $2,000 a month." And it might be true. The fact is, though, that according to a 2005 Oppenheimer Fund survey, almost 70 percent of retirees say they spend the same or *even more* than they did when they were working.[1] No wonder 98 percent of retirees regret how they spent their money before retiring! Will you have regrets like that? Do you want to wait until you retire to find out? Doesn't sound like a very good idea, does it? Fortunately, you don't have to. There's a way to find out right now how much you'll need to live on every month when you stop working.

The first thing you have to do is figure out how much your expenses are going to be and how much income you're going to have. You've already done the Lifestyle Log, so you know approximately how much you need to maintain your current lifestyle. But there are expenses that you won't have once you retire, and you can deduct them from the monthly figure. For example, if you commute to work you'll be able to deduct whatever transportation costs you every month. Similarly, if you'll have paid off your mortgage by then, or your kids will no longer require college tuition payments, you can subtract those expenses from your monthly budget.

On the other hand, you may have expenses after you retire that you don't have now. You might, for example, want to travel more or do things with your grandchildren. Perhaps you're interested in taking art or cooking courses, or even a course in financial planning!

I would caution you to not underestimate how much you need to live on. Think about what you do on the weekends when you have more free time or when you're on vacation. Does what you do typically involve spending money? Meanwhile, how much money do you spend while you're at work? The best thing to do is be conservative and assume your needs will stay the same. If you anticipate any increase in the amount of money you would spend after retirement, you'll need to add these costs in before you can come up with a reasonable estimate of how much you'll need to live on comfortably in today's dollars.

Once you've come up with a figure for your monthly expenses, the next step is to figure out how much income you're likely to have. Here's your chance to use the oppenheimer worksheets in Appendix B. It's probably easiest to start with Social Security. Hopefully, you've been receiving statements from the Social Security Administration telling you how much you'll be receiving every year. If not, here's a quick way to estimate it. (You can get the exact figures by going to www.ssa.gov or calling 800-772-1213 to request your statement.)

- If you now make under $25,000 a year, you can figure on getting $8,000 a year from Social Security.

■ If you're making between $25,000 and $40,000 it will be $12,000.

■ If your income is more than $40,000 you can expect to receive $14,500.

Now that you know how much you'll be getting from Social Security every year, you need to add in whatever other income you expect to have. This would include any pension payments, any distributions from a 401(k) or IRA, and all other investments. Once you've developed a list of all your sources of income, you can figure out how much you will have available to you yearly and every month.

Now you've got figures that closely estimate how much money you expect to need and how much you expect to be receiving in income once you've retired. How does it look? Is your estimated income more or less than your estimated expenses? Do you come out with something left over at the end of the month, or do you come up short? If you're like most people—or at least like most of my clients who have done this exercise—it probably looks to you that you're going to be all right when you retire. But remember, these are just estimates, so you can't be sure of how accurate they are. But there is a way to check these estimates against reality, and it's an exercise I call Retirement Boot Camp.

Retirement Boot Camp

Going to boot camp doesn't require you to actually go anywhere—except into the future. And how do you get there? Well, first you pick a month in which you want to go. And when you arrive at the beginning of that month, and throughout the rest of the month, you do the best you can to live on however much money you've determined you will have to live on when you retire. (You will, of course, have to fudge it a little, because you probably have some expenses today that you won't have in the future. For example, your mortgage may be paid off by then. But you should be able to take these expenses into account fairly easily.)

During the month that you're at Retirement Boot Camp you should track your spending very closely. In fact, for this month I'd like you to pay attention to every dollar you spend. That means if you like to play lotto or treat yourself to that afternoon cappuccino, you should make a record of it. During the month you should also figure out what you spend in a week when you are not at the office Monday through Friday.

Once the month is over, if you sit down and look at the records you've kept, you'll be able to determine with much greater accuracy whether you'll have enough money to live the way you want to in retirement. If you find that you were able to spend what you wanted and still had some money left over at the end of the month, congratulations! You can be fairly sure that, barring unforeseen circumstances, as long as you actually have as much money when you retire as you had while you were at Retirement Boot Camp, you'll be comfortable.

On the other hand, if you found that you came up short or you felt deprived (e.g., you missed saying yes to the friends who invited you out to dinner or for a weekend at a

B&B), you need to rethink your retirement plans. If that's the case, though, there's no reason to be embarrassed or upset. Many of my clients wash out of Retirement Boot Camp the first time they try it. They find it simply too difficult to manage their lives on the funds they've allotted. But all it means is that you need to boost your retirement savings if you want to maintain your current lifestyle after retirement.

More important, if you do the exercise now, while you're still in your active income-earning years, and discover there's a problem, you can do something about it. You still have time to boost your income, discipline your spending, strengthen your savings, and rev up your investing. The efforts you make today will compound every day from now on, so the sooner you start, the greater your rewards.

MAKING THE NET WORTH WORKOUT A HABIT FOR LIFE

If there is one thing I hope you understand by now it's that the Net Worth Workout is ultimately about bringing control to the way you handle your money. It's not a "get rich quick" type of plan, like those books that promise that "you too can become a millionaire in five easy steps on $10 a day." It's about staying focused and disciplined. It's about being persistent and making a commitment. And it's about staying the course over the long term. That's why I recommend that you track your Net Worth Statement every three months. That way you can see your net worth grow from quarter to quarter and from year to year. It gives you a perspective not only on where you've come from, but also on where you're going.

One person I know arrived in New York with $60,000 of students loans and no job. The first year he was earning $35,000 a year, barely getting by. He often had to spend Saturday nights reading, he told me, because he couldn't afford to go out with his friends for dinner. He started using the Net Worth Workout and now he owns two homes, has over $1 million in investments, and is comfortably on track to stop working when he's fifty-five. What's important is that he never thinks of himself as "having arrived." He sticks to the discipline that got him there in the first place. He continues to save 20 percent of his gross income and monitors his investments regularly, all the habits that made him financially independent. I expect that he'll do this for the rest of his life.

Of course, every person's case is different, and I can't promise that if you show up in New York owing thousands of dollars you will end up a multimillionaire. What I can promise you, though, is that if you follow the Net Worth Workout, you will understand your financial situation better than ever before; you will save more money than you ever thought possible; and you will feel confident that you are doing the most you can to ensure you will have a comfortable life, living within your means for the rest of your life.

I hope this book has helped you look at your money in a different light. I hope you have taken notes, dog-eared pages, and highlighted key points—and that you've learned it takes persistence, consistency, and active participation every day to better yourself and your family. It takes work and courage to make these positive changes permanent. But I promise you the payoff is terrific. I'm certain that by following the Net Worth Workout, you'll have more dollars in your accounts. But more important, because you won't be preoccupied or worrying about your money, you'll feel better about having more time and energy to devote to your family and friends. That change will impact your life every day, and that's what is really priceless!

NOTES

1. Oppenheimer Funds, "Investing for Retirement Survey," March 10, 2005.

BLOOMBERG

www.bloomberg.com
One of the five most visited financial websites, it's a single-source financial site for news drawing information from 1200 reporters in 85 bureaus worldwide. Along with the latest in financial news, it also has great tutorials at Bloomberg University, suitable even for the novice investor.

CNET INVESTOR

www.cnetinvestor.com
They are the leader in tech news. This site includes great information on stock splits, broker reports, the latest news from the NASDAQ, including industry Q&A, market preview, and much more.

CNNMONEY

www.money.cnn.com

This site draws from the tremendous resources of CNN and the personal finance expertise of *Money Magazine*. In addition to the latest on financial markets, it also has a good focus on personal finances, including retirement, mutual funds, and other topics to help you make the most of your money.

EDMUNDS.COM AND/OR KELLY BLUE BOOK

www.kbb.com and *www.edmunds.com*

Two very popular resources for finding used car values and new car pricing. They are great tools to learn what others are paying for new and used cars.

ED SLOTT'S IRA NEWSLETTER

www.irahelp.com

Ed Slott is a valuable resource for tax, retirement, and estate planning. It's the "go to" site for your questions on IRAs, Roths, 401(K)s, profit sharing plans—you name it—anything to do with the world of retirement planning vehicles. It has useful tables, such as the Joint Life Expectancy and Uniform Life for individuals who want to calculate minimum required distribution.

FINANCIAL ENGINES

www.financialengines.com
This site was founded by Nobel laureate William F. Sharpe and former SEC commissioner Joseph A. Grundfest. Sharpe is one of the fathers of Modern Portfolio Theory. It's particularly good for impartial 401(k) advice. It's also a good place to turn if you want advice on how to save more and create better diversification for your investments.

JPMORGAN CHASE

www.chase.com
The retail financial services within JPMorgan Chase. You can get information on mortgage rates, CDs, and auto loans, among many other things. It also offers calculators for planning your children's education, learning what you'll need to save for retirement, and refinancing your home. The site includes tools for small business owners.

MONSTER.COM

www.monster.com
This is the largest and most comprehensive job search engine on the web. It has good résumé tips, salary comparisons, and career advice. You can post your résumé, find a candidate, network, get advice (that's very targeted), and find cool community resources.

MORNINGSTAR.COM

www.morningstar.com
This mutual fund research site covers thousands of mutual funds and stocks using the well known Morningstar star rating system. It can check your holdings for unexpected risks, and provides access to Morningstar research as well as top news stories. The only drawback is that for really outstanding information, you need to subscribe.

MPOWER.COM

www.Mpower.com
An investment advisory firm that specializes in serving the large plan sponsor retirement market. It's geared to helping retirement plan participants plan for a better retirement. Morningstar's acquisition of MPower has produced a synergistic relationship that is good for both.

MSN MONEY

www.moneycentral.msn.com
Great expertise from the people at MSN and CNBC. Tons of great information to handle your personal finances, from signing up for bill pay to tracking your investments. The stock and fund screener allows you to enter criteria and search more than 10,000 companies and funds to find the investments that meet your criteria.

THE MOTLEY FOOL

www.fool.com
Their purpose is to "serve, teach you, and have a heck of a lot of fun." If you want a personal finance website with a sense of humor that can provide you with current market news, discussion boards (financial and nonfinancial), tracking your portfolio, calculators, and more, then this is your site.

THE NEW YORK STOCK EXCHANGE

www.nyse.com
This site provides daily share volume back to 1888 and daily market indices back to 1966.

PAYCHECKCITY.COM

www.paycheckcity.com
This site provides free calculators for paycheck information, bonuses, gross pay, W-4 forms, 401(k) plans, stock options, and more. What is particularly helpful is how it breaks this information down by state.

QUICKEN

www.quicken.com
This is a software tool for personal financial management. It helps you track all your financial accounts and pay bills

online. It also helps you handle your investments and taxes and make plans for your financial future.

VAULT.COM

www.vault.com
A good site for job searchers and career development. There is very useful research on companies, including employee surveys, the workplace, interviews, salaries, etc. It also has top undergrad, law, and business school surveys covering academics, quality of life, etc.

YAHOO FINANCE

www.finance.yahoo.com
One of the most popular financial websites with lots of great information. It has in-depth investing and money analysis and lots of historical data for stocks, options, major indices, and futures. It also has great community tools, such as message boards and clubs.

APPENDIX B: USEFUL FINANCIAL PLANNING TOOLS

WORKSHEET

Your Retirement

The savings you need for retirement depend on a number of factors: years until you retire, inflation, investment returns, etc. Using your best estimates, complete the worksheet below. Show it to your financial advisor, who can help you create a retirement savings strategy that suits your needs.

1	Your current annual income	$
2	Estimate the percentage of income you'll need at retirement *(usually between 75% and 100% of preretirement income)*	%
3	Multiply line 1 by line 2 for your estimated annual income retirement need	$
4	Annual Social Security benefits you expect to receive[1]	$
5	Estimated annual amount you might receive from pensions and other sources of retirement income	$
6	Subtract line 4 and line 5 from line 3 for your retirement income shortfall	$
7	From Table A, find and insert the *inflation factor* corresponding to your anticipated retirement date	x
8	Multiply line 6 by line 7 for your inflation-adjusted annual retirement income need	$
9	Multiply line 8 by the number 11 for estimated total assets needed at retirement[2]	$
10	Estimate the value of your current retirement investments, including IRAs, company retirement plans and personal savings	$
11	From Table B, find and insert the *growth factor* corresponding to your anticipated retirement date and expected rate of return	x
12	Multiply line 10 by line 11 for your estimated investment assets at retirement	$
13	Subtract line 12 from line 9 for your expected retirement savings shortfall	$
14	From Table A, find and insert the *divisor* corresponding to your expected retirement date	÷
15	Divide line 13 by line 14 for the amount you need to invest each year to achieve your retirement goal	$

Table A: Inflation & Divisor			Table B: Growth Factor			
Choose the inflation factor and divisor based on the number of years until retirement			*Choose the growth factor based on the number of years until retirement and your investments' estimated average annual rate of return*			
Years to Retirement	**Inflation Factor[3]**	**Divisor[4]**	**4% Annual Investment Return**	**6% Annual Investment Return**	**8% Annual Investment Return**	**10% Annual Investment Return**
10	1.34	14.49	1.48	1.79	2.16	2.59
20	1.81	45.76	2.19	3.21	4.66	6.73
30	2.43	113.28	3.24	5.74	10.06	17.45
40	3.26	259.06	4.80	10.29	21.72	45.26

1. Please refer to Social Security Administration website at www.ssa.gov/mystatement/index.htm.
2. Assumes 3% annual inflation, 8% investment return and 15 years spent in retirement.
3. Assumes 3% annual inflation.
4. Assumes 8% average annual return.

Source: OppenheimerFunds Distributor, Inc.

WORKSHEET

College Planning

Tuition Cost Estimate

1 Based upon when your child will begin school, enter the projected cost for four years of college (*See Table A below*). $

Savings

2 Enter the amount you've already set aside for college expenses. $

3 Subtract line 2 from line 1 and enter that number. This is the total dollar amount you'll need to save. $

Monthly Investment

4 Refer to *Table B* below and enter the number that corresponds best to your investment time horizon and how much you'll need to save (*line 3*). This is the recommended dollar amount you'll need to invest each month in order to seek your goal. It's important to remember that both college costs and investment returns are variable, so you should consider reviewing this plan periodically with your financial advisor to see if you are still on course. $

Table A. Projected College Expenses[1]

Beginning School Year	Annual Cost Public	Projected Four-year Public	Annual Cost Private	Projected Four-year Private
2004	$18,686	$79,355	$35,385	$151,241
2005	19,444	82,962	37,479	160,928
2006	20,202	86,554	39,255	168,565
2007	21,159	90,311	41,119	176,569
2008	22,077	94,240	43,074	184,956
2009	23,036	98,350	45,117	193,746
2010	24,039	102,653	47,259	202,967
2011	25,089	107,758	49,506	213,879
2012	26,187	113,744	51,864	226,650
2013	27,338	120,604	54,338	241,460
2014	29,144	128,701	58,170	258,532
2015	31,074	137,261	62,278	276,826
2016	33,138	146,413	66,682	296,438
2017	35,344	156,200	71,403	317,465
2018	37,704	166,668	76,464	340,009
2019	40,227	177,863	81,890	364,182
2020	42,925	189,839	87,708	390,103
2021	45,812	202,651	93,947	417,898

Table B. Monthly Investment Chart[2]

Time Horizon	Targeted Amount			
	$25,000	$50,000	$100,000	$250,000
18 yrs.	$ 52	$104	$ 208	$ 521
17	58	116	232	579
16	65	129	258	646
15	72	144	289	722
14	81	162	325	812
13	92	183	366	916
12	104	208	416	1,039
11	119	237	475	1,187
10	137	273	547	1,367
9	159	318	635	1,588
8	187	374	747	1,868
7	223	446	892	2,230
6	272	543	1,087	2,717
5	340	680	1,361	3,402

1. Source of chart data: *College Money,* "Annual College Cost Survey 2003." *College Money* surveyed 20 benchmark colleges in four U.S. regions and averaged total costs for each of the five categories. Average college costs include tuition, fees, room, board, books and supplies, transportation and other expenses for the 2003-2004 school year. Projected future costs are calculated using a proprietary college inflation factor developed by *College Money.*
2. These figures assume a hypothetical 8% annual return. This hypothetical chart is for illustrative purposes only and does not predict or depict the returns of any particular type of investment. Actual returns will vary. In general, mutual funds do not pay or guarantee fixed rates of return.

This worksheet contains an introduction to funding a college education. It is intended as a discussion starter for further exploration with a qualified financial, tax or legal advisor. It is not intended to provide legal, tax or investment advice, nor is it intended as a complete discussion of the tax and legal issues surrounding funding a college education.

9

Source: OppenheimerFunds Distributor, Inc.

WORKSHEET

Purchasing Your Home

This worksheet will help you calculate the amount you need to save each year to amass a 20% down payment for the purchase of a new home.

1	Cost of the home you want to buy	$
2	Years until you expect to purchase a new home	
3	Multiply line 1 by 0.20 for the amount of down payment required	$
4	Estimate your closing costs (generally 0%–3% in "points" plus other bank fees¹)	$
5	Add lines 3 and 4 for the total amount of cash required to purchase home	$
6	Current savings earmarked for home purchase	$
7	From Table A, find and insert the *growth factor* corresponding to line 2	
8	Multiply line 6 by line 7 for the estimated future value of your savings	$
9	Subtract line 8 from line 5 for your estimated future value of your savings shortfall	$
10	From Table A, find and insert the *annuitization factor* corresponding to line 2	
11	Multiply line 9 by line 10 for the amount you need to save each year to achieve your goal	$

Table A: Growth and Annuitization Factors

Years to Purchase	Growth Factor	Annuitization
1	1.000	1.000
2	1.000	0.500
3	1.060	0.327
5	1.160	0.188
10	1.480	0.083

This example assumes a 4% annual real rate of return which is composed of an 8% nominal return, less a 4% rate of inflation.

1. Can include application fee, credit report, appraisal, title transfer and other miscellaneous charges.

Source: OppenheimerFunds Distributor, Inc.

The Callan Periodic Table of Investment Returns

Annual Returns for Key Indices (1985–2004)

Ranked in order of performance (Best to Worst)

Year	1st	2nd	3rd	4th	5th	6th	7th	8th
1985	MSCI EAFE 53.14%	S&P/Barra 500 Growth 33.31%	S&P 500 31.73%	Russell 2000 31.05%	Russell 2000 Growth 31.01%	Russell 2000 Value 30.97%	S&P/Barra 500 Value 29.68%	LB Agg 22.13%
1986	MSCI EAFE 69.45%	S&P/Barra 500 Growth 21.67%	S&P 500 18.67%	LB Agg 15.30%	S&P/Barra 500 Value 14.90%	Russell 2000 7.41%	Russell 2000 Value 5.68%	Russell 2000 Growth 3.58%
1987	MSCI EAFE 24.64%	S&P/Barra 500 Growth 6.50%	S&P 500 5.25%	S&P/Barra 500 Value 3.68%	LB Agg 2.75%	Russell 2000 -7.11%	Russell 2000 Value -8.01%	Russell 2000 Growth -10.48%
1988	Russell 2000 Value 29.47%	MSCI EAFE 28.26%	Russell 2000 25.02%	S&P/Barra 500 Value 21.67%	Russell 2000 Growth 20.37%	S&P 500 Index 16.61%	S&P/Barra 500 Growth 11.95%	LB Agg 7.89%
1989	S&P/Barra 500 Growth 36.40%	S&P 500 Index 31.69%	S&P/Barra 500 Value 26.13%	Russell 2000 Growth 20.17%	Russell 2000 16.25%	LB Agg 14.53%	Russell 2000 Value 12.43%	MSCI EAFE 10.53%
1990	LB Agg 8.96%	S&P/Barra 500 Growth 0.20%	S&P 500 Index -3.11%	S&P/Barra 500 Value -6.85%	Russell 2000 Growth -17.41%	Russell 2000 -19.48%	Russell 2000 Value -21.77%	MSCI EAFE -23.45%
1991	Russell 2000 Growth 51.19%	Russell 2000 46.04%	Russell 2000 Value 41.70%	S&P/Barra 500 Growth 38.37%	S&P 500 Index 30.47%	S&P/Barra 500 Value 22.56%	LB Agg 16.00%	MSCI EAFE 12.14%
1992	Russell 2000 Value 29.14%	Russell 2000 18.41%	S&P/Barra 500 Value 10.52%	Russell 2000 Growth 7.77%	S&P 500 Index 7.62%	LB Agg 7.40%	S&P/Barra 500 Growth 5.06%	MSCI EAFE -12.18%
1993	MSCI EAFE 32.57%	Russell 2000 Value 23.77%	Russell 2000 18.90%	S&P/Barra 500 Value 18.61%	Russell 2000 Growth 13.37%	S&P 500 Index 10.08%	LB Agg 9.75%	S&P/Barra 500 Growth 1.68%
1994	MSCI EAFE 7.78%	S&P/Barra 500 Growth 3.13%	S&P 500 Index 1.32%	S&P/Barra 500 Value -0.64%	Russell 2000 Value -1.54%	Russell 2000 -1.82%	Russell 2000 Growth -2.43%	LB Agg -2.92%
1995	S&P/Barra 500 Growth 38.13%	S&P 500 Index 37.58%	S&P/Barra 500 Value 36.99%	Russell 2000 Growth 31.04%	Russell 2000 28.45%	Russell 2000 Value 25.75%	LB Agg 18.48%	MSCI EAFE 11.21%
1996	S&P/Barra 500 Growth 23.97%	S&P 500 Index 22.96%	S&P/Barra 500 Value 22.00%	Russell 2000 Value 21.37%	Russell 2000 16.49%	Russell 2000 Growth 11.26%	MSCI EAFE 6.05%	LB Agg 3.64%
1997	S&P/Barra 500 Growth 36.52%	S&P 500 Index 33.36%	Russell 2000 Value 31.78%	S&P/Barra 500 Value 29.98%	Russell 2000 22.36%	Russell 2000 Growth 12.95%	LB Agg 9.64%	MSCI EAFE 1.78%
1998	S&P/Barra 500 Growth 42.16%	S&P 500 Index 28.58%	MSCI EAFE 20.00%	S&P/Barra 500 Value 14.69%	LB Agg 8.73%	Russell 2000 Growth 1.23%	Russell 2000 -2.55%	Russell 2000 Value -6.45%
1999	Russell 2000 Growth 43.09%	S&P/Barra 500 Growth 28.24%	MSCI EAFE 26.96%	Russell 2000 21.26%	S&P 500 Index 21.04%	S&P/Barra 500 Value 12.73%	LB Agg -0.82%	Russell 2000 Value -1.49%
2000	Russell 2000 Value 22.83%	LB Agg 11.63%	S&P/Barra 500 Value 6.08%	Russell 2000 -3.02%	S&P 500 Index -9.11%	MSCI EAFE -14.17%	S&P/Barra 500 Growth -22.08%	Russell 2000 Growth -22.43%
2001	Russell 2000 Value 14.02%	LB Agg 8.43%	Russell 2000 2.49%	Russell 2000 Growth -9.23%	S&P/Barra 500 Value -11.71%	S&P 500 Index -11.89%	S&P/Barra 500 Growth -12.73%	MSCI EAFE -21.44%
2002	LB Agg 10.26%	Russell 2000 Value -11.43%	MSCI EAFE -15.94%	Russell 2000 -20.48%	S&P/Barra 500 Value -20.85%	S&P 500 Index -22.10%	S&P/Barra 500 Growth -23.59%	Russell 2000 Growth -30.26%
2003	Russell 2000 Growth 48.54%	Russell 2000 47.25%	Russell 2000 Value 46.03%	MSCI EAFE 38.59%	S&P/Barra 500 Value 31.79%	S&P 500 Index 28.68%	S&P/Barra 500 Growth 25.66%	LB Agg 4.10%
2004	Russell 2000 Value 22.25%	MSCI EAFE 20.25%	Russell 2000 18.33%	S&P/Barra 500 Value 15.71%	Russell 2000 Growth 14.31%	S&P 500 Index 10.88%	S&P/Barra 500 Growth 6.13%	LB Agg 4.34%

S&P 500 Index measures the performance of large capitalization U.S. stocks. The S&P 500 is a market-value-weighted index of 500 stocks that are traded on the NYSE, AMEX and NASDAQ. The weightings make each company's influence on the Index performance directly proportional to that company's market value.

S&P/Barra 500 Growth and **S&P/Barra 500 Value** Index indices measure the performance of growth and value styles of investing in large cap U.S. stocks. The indices are constructed by dividing the stocks in the S&P 500 Index according to price-to-book ratios. The Growth index contains stocks with higher price-to-book ratios. The Value index contains stocks with lower price-to-book ratios. The indices are market-capitalization-weighted and their constituents are mutually exclusive.

Russell 2000 Index measures the performance of small capitalization U.S. stocks. The Russell 2000 is a market-value-weighted index of the 2,000 smallest stocks in the broad-market Russell 3000 Index. These securities are traded on the NYSE, AMEX and NASDAQ.

Russell 2000 Value and **Russell 2000 Growth** indices measure the performance of growth and value styles of investing in small cap U.S. stocks. The Value index contains those Russell 2000 securities with a less-than-average growth orientation, while the Growth index contains those securities with a greater-than-average growth orientation. Securities in the Value index generally have lower price-to-book and price-earnings ratios than those in the Growth index. The constituent securities are NOT mutually exclusive.

MSCI EAFE is a Morgan Stanley Capital International index that is designed to measure the performance of the developed stock markets of Europe, Australasia and the Far East.

LB Agg is the Lehman Brothers Aggregate Bond Index. This index includes U.S. government, corporate and mortgage-backed securities with maturities of at least one year.

CALLAN ASSOCIATES

© 2005 Callan Associates Inc.

CALLAN ASSOCIATES INC.

The Callan Periodic Table of Investment Returns (1985–2004)

The Callan Periodic Table of Investment Returns conveys an enormous amount of information. Above all, the Table shows that the **case for diversification,** across investment styles (growth vs. value), capitalization (large vs. small) and equity markets (U.S. vs. international) is strong.

While past performance is no indication of the future, consider the following observations:

- The Table illustrates the unique experience of the 1995–1999 period, when **large cap growth** significantly outperformed all other asset classes and the U.S. stock market in general enjoyed one of its strongest five-year runs.

- The subsequent three years (2000–2002) saw consecutive declines in **large cap stocks** for the first time since 1929–32. The S&P 500 suffered its largest loss since 1974, declining 40% from the market peak in March 2000 through the end of 2002.

- The stock market moderated substantially in 2004 after the tremendous gains in 2003. Returns on large cap and **international stocks** fell by almost 20 percentage points, while returns for small cap were approximately 30 percentage points lower. Despite the lower returns, 2004 was the second year in a row in which all of the asset categories depicted on the Table enjoyed positive returns.

- 2004 marked the sixth year in a row that **small cap stocks** outperformed large cap. **Small cap value** topped the performance rankings among all asset categories, with international equity coming in a close second. While the purpose of the Table is to compare relative rather than absolute performance, it should be noted that the equity rankings barely changed from 2003 while the level of equity returns slowed dramatically. The 22.25% gain in small cap value was lower than the 25.66% return in large cap growth in 2003, which ranked **last** among equity categories that year.

- Value outperformed growth in both large and small cap equity markets during 2004. The huge disparity in performance between the two styles, seen during 1997–2000 for large cap and from 1996–2002 for small cap, has disappeared.

- **Fixed income** ranked last in 2004 for the second year in a row, after ranking first in 2002 and second during the two previous years. The surprise for many investors was not that fixed income lagged stocks, but that it recorded a positive return at all, given the rising interest rate environment. The Federal Reserve raised interest rates five times during 2004, boosting the Federal Funds rate by 1.25%.

- The Table highlights the **uncertainty** inherent in all capital markets. Rankings change every year. Also noteworthy is the difference between absolute and relative performance. For example, witness the variability of returns for international equity when it ranked last for four straight years 1989–1992, or for large cap growth, when it ranked second from last for the past five years.

This analysis assumes that market indices are reasonable representations of the asset classes and depict the returns an investor could expect from exposure to these styles of investment. In fact, investment manager performance relative to the different asset class indices has varied widely across the asset classes during the past 20 years.

Please visit our website for our quarterly Capital Market Review newsletter containing our commentary on changes in the capital markets (www.callan.com – click on the "resource center" and "periodicals").

Callan Associates offers a full range of consulting services to corporate pension and profit-sharing plans, multi-employer plans, endowments and foundations, public pension plans, high net-worth individuals, and investment management organizations.

To learn more about our services, check our website (www.callan.com) or contact our office headquarters:

Callan Associates Inc.
101 California Street, Suite 3500
San Francisco, CA 94111
Tel: 415.974.5060
Fax: 415.291.4014

Note: A printable copy of The Callan Periodic Table of Investment Returns is available on our website at www.callan.com/resource/.

adjusted gross income (AGI)   Used to determine how much of your income is taxable. AGI consists of gross income from taxable sources minus your maximum allowable adjustments.

asset   A resource having economic value that an individual or business entity owns or controls with the expectation that it will provide future benefit.

asset allocation   This is a strategy advocated by modern portfolio theory for maximizing gain while minimizing risk in an investment portfolio. It entails dividing your assets among different broad categories of investment, including stocks, bonds, and cash. The percentages depend on factors such as risk tolerance, time horizon, and market outlook.

behavioral finance   An attempt to provide a framework for understanding the behavior of investors and the markets in which they invest. It holds that investors sometimes are not totally rational beings, that they sometimes act on imperfect or incomplete information and may misinterpret information or react to it in inappropriate ways. Behaviorists believe the nonrational behaviors of investors sometimes fall into patterns that can be predictable.

bond   A debt instrument that pays back cash to the holder at regular intervals. This payment is usually a fixed percentage normally known as a *coupon*. At maturity the face value of the bond is usually paid back.

Bonds are issued by the U.S. government, state governments, local governments, corporations, and foreign countries. Many other types of institutions also sell bonds.

compounding   The ability of an asset to generate earnings that are then added to principal and reinvested to generate their own earnings.

corporate bond   A debt issued by a corporation as opposed to debt issued by a government.

cost basis   The original principal one invests, plus any dividends and capital gains that get reinvested and have already been taxed.

defined benefit plan   Pension and target benefit plans that promise to pay retired employees specific dollar benefits based on a formula such as salary and years of service.

defined contribution plan   Profit sharing, 401(k), and money purchase plans in which retirement benefits are based on the amount of contributions and the investment performance of the plan. There is no way to know the amount of benefit the plan will ultimately give the employee in retirement. The amount of contribution is fixed but the benefit is not.

deferred annuity   A type of annuity contract that delays payments of income (installments or a lump sum) until the investor elects to receive the funds. This type of annuity has two main phases: the savings phase, in which you invest money into the account, and the income phase, in which the plan is converted into an annuity and payments, either fixed or variable, are paid out to the investor.

disability insurance   Insurance that protects one's income should that person become ill or injured. An employee purchases this insurance, or a company on the employee's behalf, and pays premiums. If the insured person cannot work because of illness or injury, the insurance company then pays a portion of salary, typically 60 to 70 percent of the person's gross income.

dividend   A distribution of a portion of a company's earnings to a class of its shareholders. Dividend decisions are made by the board of directors. The amount of a dividend is expressed in per-share terms, e.g., 2 cents per share.

dollar cost averaging   The technique of buying a fixed dollar amount of a particular investment on a regular schedule. The objective is to even out the cost among shares purchased when prices are low and shares purchased when prices are high.

529 Education Plan   A plan whereby individuals can contribute (double for married couples) to a state-sponsored higher education savings program on behalf of a designated beneficiary (including themselves). The contributions are considered gifts and grow tax deferred. Funds withdrawn for qualified education expenses such as tuition, fees, room, and board are free of federal taxes and most states don't tax the earnings. If the funds are not used for higher education, the funds are subject to taxes and penalties.

401(k)   The 401(k) is a defined contribution plan that allows employees to defer up to 100 percent of their compensation, pre-tax, per year. (Currently, the law permits a $15,000 maximum contribution, plus a "catch-up provision" of $5,000 for employees over age 50.) Also, the plan may permit up to 10 percent after-tax contributions. Employers may voluntarily match employee contributions, but the combined total of all contributions cannot exceed $42,000.

403(b)   This employer-sponsored savings plan is for employees of not-for-profit organizations, such as colleges, hospitals, and cultural organizations. Contributions are tax deductible, earnings are tax deferred, and annual contribution limits are similar to 401(k) plans.

457 Plan   This tax-deferred retirement savings plan was designed for state and municipal employees. As with 403(b) and 401(k) plans, earnings are not taxed until withdrawals are made, usually at retirement. Unlike other plans, contributions are completely funded by the employee, and the annual contribution cap is somewhat lower than for the 401(k).

government security   A government debt obligation backed by the credit and taxing power of the entity issuing it. Government securities carry less risk of default.

growth stock   Shares in a company whose earnings are expected to grow at an above-average rate relative to the market.

guaranteed investment contract (GIC)   Insurance contracts that guarantee the owner a fixed or floating interest rate for a predetermined period of time.

home equity loan   A consumer loan secured by a second mortgage allowing homeowners to borrow against the equity in their homes. The loan is based on the difference between the homeowner's equity and the home's current market value. The mortgage also provides collateral for an asset backed security issued by the lender and sometimes tax deductible interest payments for the borrower. It's also known as an "equity loan" or a "second mortgage."

inflation   The economic condition of rising prices for goods and services. The average historical rate of inflation is 3 percent.

large cap   A company with a market capitalization of between $10 billion and $200 billion, for example, JPMorgan, Microsoft, and General Electric.

liability   A legal debt or obligation estimated via accrual accounting. For example, liabilities include loans, credit card debt, and mortgages.

lump-sum distribution   This is the payment of all funds from the same type of qualified employer retirement plan to a plan participant in the same taxable year. If the person belongs to more than one plan and the funds are distributed in the same year, it is considered one lump-sum distribution. To qualify as a lump-sum, the funds must be distributed due to one of four events: death, permanent disability, attainment of age 59½ (if the plan allows), or separation of service.

Medicaid   A joint federal and state program that helps low-income individuals or families pay for the costs associated with long-term medical and custodial care, provided they qualify. Although largely funded by the federal government, Medicaid is run by the states; therefore coverage may vary.

Medicare   A U.S. federal health-care program that subsidizes people who meet one of the following criteria: (1) an individual over the age of 65 who has been a U.S. citizen or permanent legal resident for five years; (2) an individual who is disabled and has collected social security for a minimum of two years; (3) an individual who is undergoing dialysis for kidney failure; (4) an individual who has ALS, or Lou Gehrig's disease.

mental accounting An economic theory established by economist Richard Thaler which contends that individuals divide their current and future assets into separate nontransferable portions. The theory purports that individuals assign different levels of utility to each asset group, which affects their consumption decisions and behavior.

mid cap A stock with a market cap of between $2 billion and $10 billion.

mortgage A loan, typically by a bank, secured by the collateral of a specific piece of real estate. The borrower is obligated to make specific payments at specific times.

municipal bond A debt security issued by a state, municipality, or county to finance its capital expenditures. Municipal bonds are exempt from federal taxes and from most state and local taxes, especially if you live in the state where the bond is issued.

mutual fund A pool of money from many investors managed by an investment company for the purpose of buying various kinds of investments (stocks, bonds, and or cash equivalents). There are mutual funds to fit most any type of investment style, risk-tolerance profile, and goal. They are regulated by the Investment Company Act of 1940.

net worth The value of assets a person owns, including home, securities, personal property, retirement accounts, and the like, minus liabilities (e.g., loans and other obligations). If assets exceed liabilities, net worth is said to be positive. If liabilities outweigh assets, one's net worth is negative.

opportunity cost The cost of an alternative that must be foregone in order to pursue a certain investing action. The difference in return between an investment that is chosen and one that is necessarily passed up. For example, the opportunity cost of going to college is the money you would have earned had you worked instead.

option   A financial instrument that allows investors to either buy or sell a specified quantity of an "underlying investment" (stocks, stock indexes, government debt, foreign currencies) at a predetermined price within a specified time period. Options may be used by hedgers and speculators because they provide great leverage of the underlying security. Options themselves and their strategies can be structurally complex, and they have relatively short expiration periods. They are suitable only for sophisticated investors.

pension plan   A retirement plan, usually tax exempt, wherein the employer makes contributions for the employee. Most of these plans are being replaced by 401(k) and other defined contribution plans.

portfolio   The group of investments, such as stocks, bonds, and mutual funds, that are held by an investor.

proxy directive   A legal document assigning the responsibility to make health-care decisions to another person in the event the assigning individual is unable to make such decisions for himself or herself.

real rate of return   The annual percentage return realized on an investment, adjusted for changes in prices due to inflation or deflation.

real estate investment trust (REIT)   A security that sells like a stock on the major exchanges and invests in real estate directly, even through property or mortgages. REITs receive special tax considerations and typically offer investors high yields as well as a highly liquid method of investing in real estate.

Roth IRA   A Roth IRA is available to those who qualify based on their income. It is a retirement account that allows contributors to make annual contributions of after-tax funds. Earnings accumulate tax free, and contributors may withdraw the principal and earnings tax free after they reach $59\frac{1}{2}$.

Rule of 72   A rule stating that in order to find the number of years required to double your money at a given interest rate, you divide the compound return into 72. The result is the approximate amount of time it will take to double your money.

S&P 500 (Standard and Poor's 500 Index) An index consisting of 500 stocks chosen for market size, liquidity, and industry group representation, among other factors. It is designed to be a leading indicator of U.S. equities and is meant to reflect the risk/return characteristics of the large cap universe.

SEP-IRA The Simplified Employee Pension IRA. A low-cost and easy-to-administer retirement plan for self-employed individuals, partnerships, and small "S" or "C" corporations. The employers can make discretionary contributions up to 25 percent of compensation ($42,000 maximum) to each employee's account. The plan must include all employees who are 21 years old and have earned $450 or more in at least three of the previous five years.

SIMPLE IRA This stands for the Savings Incentive Match Plan for Employees for employers with 100 or fewer employees who have earned at least $5000 in the last two prior years. Eligible employees can elect to contribute up to 100 percent of their compensation up to $10,000 per year. The employer must match contributions dollar for dollar up to 3 percent of pay or contribute 2 percent of pay for all eligible employees regardless of elective deferrals. There are no annual 5500 filings or ADP/top heavy testing, and employees are 100 percent vested.

small cap A stock with a relatively small market capitalization, generally from $300 million to $2 billion.

stock Ownership of a corporation, indicated by shares which represent a piece of the corporation's assets and earnings.

term life insurance A policy with a death benefit and set duration limit on the coverage period. Once the time limit expires, it is up to the policyholder to decide whether to renew the coverage or let it terminate. There is no savings component as with permanent (or whole life) insurance. It is less expensive than permanent insurance.

traditional IRA An individual retirement account to which workers under the age of 70½ may contribute 100 percent of earned income up to $4,000. Individuals who reach age 50 before year's end may contribute an extra $1,000. In 2008, the maximum will increase to $5,000 and will be adjusted for inflation thereafter. Normally, contributions must be made by April 15ᵗʰ of the year following the tax year for which the contribution is made. The funds grow tax deferred until they're withdrawn. If the individual is also covered by a qualified plan, such as a 401(k), the deductibility of contributions will depend on the person's tax filing status and adjusted gross income (AGI).

12b 1 Fee   Fees a mutual fund company levies on funds to offset the costs of promotion and marketing. These asset-based fees typically run between .25 percent and 1 percent annually of the net assets in the fund.

value stock   A stock that tends to trade at a lower price relative to its fundamentals (i.e., dividends, earnings, and sales) and therefore is considered undervalued by its investor. Some typical characteristics include a high dividend yield, low price-to-book ratio, and/or low price-to-earnings yield.

whole life insurance   A life insurance contract with level premiums that has both an insurance and an investment component. The insurance will pay a stated amount of benefit at the death of the insured. The investment component accumulates a cash value that the policyholder can withdraw or borrow against.

W2 Form   The form that an employer must send to the IRS and each employee at the end of the year reporting the employee's annual wages and the amount of taxes withheld from his or her paycheck.

INDEX

activation energy, 30
active income
    defined, 74–75
    importance of, 76–79
    maximizing, 82–85
appreciating assets, 44
asset allocation, *see* diversification
assets
    analyzing, 45–47
    defined, 44
    types of, 44
attitude, 17–39
    emotions and, 18, 37
    fight talk and, 38–39
    "flow" and, 29–33, 184
    increasing financial intelligence, 19–21
    toward change, 37–38
    toward opportunity cost, 23–27, 93
    toward prosperity as process, 34–37
    toward risk, 18–19, 154–155
    toward time, 21–23

Beebower, Gilbert, 166–167
Belsky, Gary, 158
benefits packages
    analyzing, 5–6, 78–79
    maximizing, 85–89
Bonfire of the Vanities, The (Wolfe), 96–97
bonuses, 83–84
Brinson, Gary, 166–167

cash balance pension plans, 142–143
certificates of deposit (CDs), 140
change, attitude toward, 37–38

child-care benefits, 86, 87
Citicorp, 12
college 529 plans, 143
college funds, 88, 143–144
commitment, to prosperity as process, 34–37
company-match programs, 86, 135, 160–161, 176
comparisons to others, 52–53, 84
compound interest, 22, 153–154
convenience-driven spending, 121
Coverdell education savings accounts (ESAs), 144
credit cards, 48, 60, 93, 94, 109, 187–188
Csikszentmihalyi, Mihalyi, 30

defined-benefit plans, 142–143
defined-contribution plans, 159
depreciating assets, 44
disability insurance, 77
discipline, forms of, 36
discretionary expenses, 6–7, 100–104, 108, 109, 115, 119–120, 122–124
diversification, 9, 165–173
    advantages of, 166–169, 170–171
    determining level of, 171–173
    pitfalls of, 169–170
divorce, 175–176
dollar-cost averaging, 155–159
dreams, goals versus, 59–60

earning, 4–6, 71–89
    active income, 74–75, 76–79, 82–85
    actual dollar amount of, 82–85

earning (*continued*)
  assessing, 79–82
  benefits and, 78–79, 85–89
  creating income from income, 73–74
  gross income, 80–81, 134–135
  income analysis, 80–85
  net income, 80–81
  passive income, 75, 76–77
  portfolio income, 75–77
Edison, Thomas, 36
education plans, 88, 143–144
Einstein, Albert, 153
emotions
  attitude and, 18, 37
  investing and, 167
  spending and, 102–104, 121
employee stock ownership plans (ESOPs),
    159
Ernst & Young, 130
expectations of others, 54
expenses, *see* spending

fear, of investing, 31
financial checkup, *see* goals; plans; shape
financial intelligence, increasing, 19–21
fixed expenses, 98–99, 106, 108, 115,
    123
flexible spending accounts (FSAs), 87
"flow", going for, 29–33, 184
Ford, Henry, 36
401(k) plans, 141–142, 159–161
403(b) plans, 159–161, 164
457 plans, 159–161
free agent syndrome, 83–84

gift taxes, 144–145
Gilovich, Thomas, 158
goal planner, 65–67
goals, 51–63
  defined, 41
  dreams versus, 59–60
  establishing, 51–52
  false goals, 52–55
  financial aspect of, 60–63
  flexibility of, 117
  immediate gratification and, 68–70
  keeping on track, 67–70
  long-term, 62, 64, 128, 129
  meaningful, 56–59
  medium-term, 62, 64, 129
  meeting, 119–124
  Net Worth Workout and, 13
  setting, 114–119

short-term, 61, 64, 129
  spending, 111, 114–124
  true goals, 55–60
  values versus, 55–56, 57, 60
Great Spending Riddle, 95–98
gross income, 80–81, 134–135

health-care benefits, 86, 87
hedging strategies, 77
Highest Goal, The (Ray), 58
Hood, Randolph, 166–167

immediate gratification, 68–70
impulse spending, 102–104
income, *see* earning
individual retirement accounts (IRAs),
    141–143, 159
  rollover accounts, 177
  Roth IRAs, 88, 141, 142, 161–163,
    194
  traditional IRAs, 142, 159
inflation
  retirement and, 164–165, 195–196
  Rule of 72 and, 195–196
  saving and, 130–131, 135–136, 140
insurance
  disability, 77
  life, 177
interest, compound, 22, 153–154
internalization, 11
investing, 4, 8–9, 30–31, 149–178
  compound interest and, 22, 153–154
  diversification and, 9, 165–173
  dollar-cost averaging, 155–159
  emotions and, 167
  fear and, 31
  Investment Inventory, 150–152
  tax deferral and, 163–165
  tax reduction and, 159–163
  women and, 174–178
  see also risk
IRAs, *see* individual retirement accounts
    (IRAs)

Jordan, Michael, 36
JPMorganChase, 12

Kentucky Fried Chicken, 36

Leaky Wallet Syndrome, 110–114
liabilities
  analyzing, 45–47
  defined, 44

life insurance, 177
Lifestyle Log, 104–114, 115, 119, 123–124, 132, 135, 185–186, 196–197
liquid assets, 44
long-term goals, 62, 64, 128, 129, *see also* goals; saving
loss-aversion effect, 154–155
Lucent Technologies, 169
Lusardi, Annamaria, 19–20

marketing, impact of, 101–102
medium-term goals, 62, 64, 129, *see also* goals; saving
Millionaire Mind, The (Stanley), 23, 102
Millionaire Next Door, The, 21, 22
money market accounts, 141
Morningstar.com, 151, 172

National Health and Nutrition Examination Survey, 1
net income, 80–81
Net Worth Statement, 42–51
    assessing, 47–50, 80
    assets and, 44–46
    customizing, 50 51
    form for, 46
    liabilities and, 44–47
    quarterly review of, 45, 186–190, 200 201
    sample, 48–50
    saving and, 132
    strengths and weaknesses exercise and, 188–190
Net Worth Workout
    adapting, 9–14
    expectations for, 14–16
    financial checkup in, *see* goals; plans; shape
    as habit for life, 200–202
    as ongoing "self-improvement" process, 35
    preparation for, 103–105
    in preparing for retirement, 193–200
    realistic approach to, 190–191
    Retirement Boot Camp and, 198–200
    synergy in, 180–183
    tough times and, 191–193
    two-hour millionaire's workout, 27–34
    wealth quadrants in, 3–9, *see also* earning; investing; saving; spending
nonliquid assets, 44

Oppenheimer, 62, 210–212
opportunity cost, 23–27, 93

passive income
    defined, 75
    as "magical," 76–77
Pension Maximization (Pension Max), 177
pension plans, 142–143, 159, 175, 176–177
plans, 63–67
    defined, 42
    procrastination and, 63–65, 130–131
portfolio income
    defined, 75–76
    as "magical," 76–77
priorities
    goals and, 62
    personal memories and, 51
    spending and, 111, 114–124
procrastination, 63–65, 130, 131
profit-sharing plans, 159, 164
prosperity, as process, 34–37

Ray, Michael, 58
reference anxiety, 52–53, 84
retirement plans
    401(k) plans, 141–142, 159–161
    403(b) plans, 159–161, 164
    457 plans, 159–161
    funding, 88
    inflation and, 164–165, 195–196
    money needed for retirement and, 194, 196–198
    Net Worth Workout and, 193 200
    pension plans and, 142–143, 159, 175, 176–177
    Retirement Boot Camp and, 198–200
    saving with, 131, 137, 141–143
    self-employment and, 159, 164
    Social Security and, 176, 197–198
    tax reduction and, 159–163
    underfunded, 2
risk
    attitude toward, 18–19, 154–155
    minimizing, 170
    opportunity cost and, 23–27, 93
    tolerance for, 167
rollover IRAs, 177
Roth IRAs, 88, 141, 142, 161–163, 194
Rule of 72, 195–196
Ruth, Babe, 36

safety net or cushion, 8, 128, 135
salary range, 82–84
Sanders, Colonel Harlan, 36

Save More Tomorrow, 137–138, 156
saving, 4, 7–8, 127–148
  actual level of, 132–134
  coordinating with other quadrants,
    145–148
  difficulty of, 129–131
  goals and, 128, 129
  importance of, 128–129
  inflation and, 130–131, 135–136, 140
  optimal level of, 134–136
  safety net for, 8, 128, 135
  savings plan for, 136–138
  savings vehicles for, 138–145
  taxes and, 130–131, 141–145
  women and, 134–135
savings accounts, 139–140
self-employment
  as goal, 10
  retirement plans and, 159, 164
setbacks, in financial plans, 14
shape, 42–51
  defined, 41
  Net Worth Statement and, 42–51
short-term goals, 61, 64, 129, *see also*
    goals; saving
simplified employee pension (SEP) plans,
    159, 164
Social Security, 176, 197–198
spending, 4, 6–7, 91–125
  discretionary expenses and, 6–7, 100–
    104, 108, 109, 115, 119–120,
    122–124
  fixed expenses and, 98–99, 106, 108,
    115, 123
  goals for, 111, 114–124
  Great Spending Riddle and, 95–98
  impulse, 102–104, 121
  Leaky Wallet Syndrome and, 110–114,
    115
  Lifestyle Log and, 104–114, 115, 119,
    123–124, 132, 135, 185–186,
    196–197
  marketing and, 101–102
  priorities and, 111, 114–124
  purchase types and, 92–95
  Spending Hangover Test, 120–121,
    122
  Spending Rule of Thumb and, 94–95,
    118, 186
  typical, 119

variable expenses and, 99–104, 107,
    109, 115, 116, 119–120, 122–124
Stanley, Thomas J., 23, 102
stress
  procrastination and, 63
  stress/spending paradox and, 102–104,
    121
  working through, 32
synergy, power of, 180–183

taxes
  deferring, 163–165
  reducing, 159–163
  on retirement plan withdrawals,
    194–195
  saving and, 130–131, 141–145
Thaler, Richard, 137–138, 168
time, 21–23
  to handle money, 22–23
  to think about finances, 21
time value of money, 22, 153–154
trading up, 93
transportation benefits, 86, 87
Trump, Donald, 36
Tufts University, 73

UGMA (Uniform Gift to Minors Act),
    144–145
University of Michigan, 2
UTMA (Uniform Transfer to Minors Act),
    144–145

values, goals versus, 55–56, 57, 60
variable expenses, 99–104, 107, 109, 115,
    116, 119–120, 122–124

wealth
  four quadrants of, 3–9
  as function of information and effort,
    20–21
  prosperity as process and, 34–37
  *Why Smart People Make Big Money Mis-
    takes* (Belsky and Gilovich), 158
  Winner vs. Loser exercise, 146–148
Wolfe, Tom, 96–97
women
  investing and, 174–178
  saving and, 134–135
WorldCom, 169
worry, freedom from, 54–55